QUIET
JOURNEY

QUIET
JOURNEY

UNDERSTANDING THE RIGHTS
OF DEAF CHILDREN

JOANNE S. CRIPPS

Cover art by Douglas Donald
Design by Lori Ledingham

Canadian Cataloguing in Publication Data

Cripps, Joanne S.
  Quiet journey: understanding the rights of deaf children

Includes bibliographical references.
ISBN 0-921773-52-8

1. Deaf children. 2. Children's rights. I.Title.

HV2391.C74 2000   362.4'2'083   C00-931136-X

Published by
The Ginger Press, Inc.
848 Second Avenue East
Owen Sound, Ontario
Canada N4K 2H3
www.gingerpress.com

Printed in Canada.

Copyright and permissions information is found on page 153.

Thank you, Mossie,
for bringing back family values

NOTE TO THE READER

I feel it is important to define a term which will be encountered throughout this book. It is common for authors to use "Deaf" with a capital "D" when discussing individuals who are members of the Deaf community and consider themselves to be culturally Deaf; while "deaf" with a lower case "d" describes an audiological state of being. I have decided not to make this distinction and use capital "D" in every use of the word Deaf.

This is not to place a particular identity on particular individuals. Rather, it is to indicate that Deaf culture is the birthright of every Deaf individual by virtue of their having been born Deaf or having become Deaf in child-hood, whether or not they have been exposed to Deaf culture. This is in keeping with how individuals from other cultural groups (such as Blacks or Jews) spell their names, regardless of the strength of their identity. I do not make assumptions about each individual's identity for them by determining whether or not their culture should begin with a capital letter.

ACKNOWLEDGMENTS

I would like to thank everyone for their support in this book. In addition to those mentioned in the text, I would like to thank: Helen Pizzacalla and Anita Small who encouraged me to continue and often acted as my sounding boards; Heather Hawthorn for volunteering to interpret between the editors and me when we discussed this book; Lisa Daudjee, John Varden and Cy Strom for editing; and Dave Mason, Heather Gibson, Julia Landau and Les Horne for their feedback.

I would also like to thank my family – Daryl, Jamey and the rest for patiently waiting while wondering if this book would ever be published. I give special thanks to Jim, my lifelong friend and husband, and to my kids, Jason and Jeri.

CONTENTS

FOREWORD

AS THE PARENT of a Deaf child, I found that little
help was available to me when Joanne was very
young. Looking back after reading this book, I
realize how different her life could have been. Neither
American Sign Language (ASL) nor natural sign language
were available to us at that time. I remember that we were
told not to spank Joanne until she understood what she
was being spanked for. Well, by the time she understood
why she was being spanked, she was too old to get a spank-
ing. So you can see how slow our communication was!

I am proud of this book. It is the true story of how the
world is for the many who can't hear. If you are the parent
of a Deaf child, you will no doubt benefit from reading this
book and realize a little more what your child is feeling
and what resources are available to you.

The truth often hurts but you cannot argue with it. If
the information presented in this book helps just one parent, it's worth it. Parents will be amazed at what their
child can accomplish with help, nurturing and encouragement along the way.

JOANNE S. CRIPPS

I asked my daughter Beth, the oldest of our six children, to share her views. Here is her response:

> Being a sister of a Deaf person has brought many different experiences and emotions to my life. When we were younger, sign language was not permitted and, at that time, the resources to learn signing were not what they are today. By not being able to communicate fully with Joanne, we all missed something in our lives. We are a close family but you need to have easy access to communication in order for all family members to be involved.
>
> Perhaps I did not realize this until one day I was looking after Joanne's ten-month-old son who is hearing. He was trying to sign something to me and I had no understanding of what he was trying to say. I felt very frustrated and I know he was feeling the same way.
>
> My Deaf sister has shown tremendous determination and drive to make a better place for Deaf people and to foster understanding of Deaf people in the hearing community. As her siblings, we are all very proud of Joanne's accomplishments. Watching her take on these obstacles and challenges pushes us to do better in our lives.

I could not have put it any better myself.

Alice G. Stephens

PREFACE

MAKE NO MISTAKE about it – Deaf people have a distinct culture. The term culturally Deaf refers to those who: are born Deaf or become Deaf at a very early age; regularly interact with Deaf adults and children; attend or have attended provincial or state schools for Deaf students; and choose ASL as their first language. These distinctions become particularly important when we consider that Deaf culture often lacks one feature that other minority cultures enjoy – the capacity to transmit language, beliefs and traditions from parent to child. More than 90 percent of Deaf children are born to hearing parents, most of whom are not able, based on lack of experience and training, to introduce their children to Deaf culture. Therefore, to truly internalize Deaf culture, a Deaf child must associate with other Deaf children and Deaf adults.

With these premises concerning Deaf culture in mind, it is important to recognize and respect the rights of Deaf children. Deaf children deserve all the rights that hearing children enjoy; however, in order for Deaf children to participate in these rights, additional prerequisite rights must be imposed to allow such opportunities. While Deaf members can clearly be contributing partners in their hearing communities, it is rare for the hearing community to be equipped for Deaf members to be active leaders in their hearing communities (Gary Malkowski, first elected Deaf MPP, 1990, is an exception). The distinctions are found in the degree of participation and quality of participation. There are still many barriers for Deaf leadership to occur in the hearing community. Therefore, the right for a Deaf child to be exposed to the Deaf community as well as the hearing community becomes essential from the point of view of the community being accessible to the Deaf child (or adult), for the community to be able to gain fully from the potential leadership abilities of the Deaf child or adult and from the perspective of the growing Deaf child who deserves the right to lead and not just take part as they develop their skills in citizenry. It is their right to actively participate and not simply contribute.

Other rights for Deaf children include: the right to clear communication access (a visual language such as a Deaf sign language may be the most accessible and naturally acquired language); the right to develop an identity and explore a culture and language that is his or her birthright; the right to know, accept and appreciate his or her own social background and the implications it has on his or her life; the right to a nurturing, caring home environment that allows for Deaf heritage; the right to know about and use visual technology that allows a Deaf child to participate equally in life in the same way a hearing child does; the right to access information about himself or herself as well as the information that is available to all people; the right to privacy; the right to equal standards in education; and the right to equal standards in the justice system.

Deaf children have the right to be themselves and to experience the natural process of child development. All children develop through stages. Deaf children, however, if deprived of the opportunity to reach the various stages due to, for example, communication "problems" cannot progress to further stages. All babies, hearing and Deaf, start to babble around six months of age. To develop babbling further into language-specific sounds, infants need to hear human speech. Research has shown (Petitto and Marentette, 1991) that Deaf infants, when exposed to signed languages also babble, but with their hands, in the same way hearing children do through speech.

I want to share with you part of a letter written by the father of a Deaf child:

> As I look back at the start of the reorganizing of our lives related to Molly's deafness, I am struck by an incredible irony. While investigating all of the available programs for Molly, we wound up at the [Oral Center in a large city,] where we were promptly told by the Director that starting Molly off with sign language was a bad idea. She informed us that if Molly learned sign language, she would never learn to speak and that we would lose our daughter to "the Deaf culture." Sounds like a plague of some kind, doesn't it? The Director's comments didn't make sense to us and we are pursuing sign language as Molly's first language.
>
> The irony is that it has taken exposure to Deaf culture to create a spark of interest in Molly. It has made her a happier child and improved her communication skills. I can tell the difference

in her from one day to the next. As a hearing parent, by hoping that Molly could be something she isn't – a hearing child who speaks – I had forgotten who she is – a great Deaf kid who for two-and-a-half years struggled and did not understand speech. Now with limited exposure to sign language, Molly seems to understand and brightens when we sign to her. I don't think I'll lose my child to the Deaf culture. In fact, Deaf culture has helped me find my child.

A Deaf child who is deprived of Deaf culture lacks the opportunity to experience, feel and appreciate a way of life that many have excelled in. By exposing their Deaf children to Deaf culture, parents do not give up their own culture, values and traditions. Rather the child learns how to balance both cultures as do immigrants to a new country. Much like new immigrants who are not exposed to their new culture feel isolated, so too will Deaf children who are deprived of knowing Deaf culture feel isolated. There could be no one with whom they can either communicate clearly or identify.

We must remember that our children are the keepers of our future. As such, Deaf children are a valuable resource for both the Deaf community and the larger hearing society. In order to help our children become responsible citizens, we must value and encourage respect for individual rights. Deaf children deserve the same attention and care as any child.

If you have ever been in a position of trust with Deaf children and felt the responsibility to inform, inspire and empower them, this book will help you. It will help you understand Deaf children's rights and, with that understanding, clarify what you can do to protect those rights.

QUIET JOURNEY

The United Nations has already determined the importance of protecting the world's most valuable resources by developing the United Nations Convention on the Rights of the Child. As Article 30 states, "In those states in which ethnic, religious or linguistic minorities ... exist, a child belonging to such a minority ... shall not be denied the right, in community with other members of his or her group, to enjoy his or her own culture, to profess and practise his or her own religion, or to use his or her own language." Although the Convention was not written with Deaf children at the forefront of its concerns, I believe that the rights assigned to minority culture children are equally applicable to the children of Deaf culture. Both represent a linguistic and cultural minority. Thus, throughout this book, I will be extending the United Nations Convention to include the rights of Deaf children. In the following chapters I will explain how the Convention's rights apply to Deaf children. When parents understand the rights of their Deaf children they are better able to respect them.

It is my hope that this book will help parents realize that they have a responsibility to advocate for equal rights for their Deaf children. Being Deaf is not a choice and therefore communication must not be made into a choice. My intention is to provide insight and background information about a culture, a language and a way of life, all of which may have been overlooked because true communication access has never before been fully explained.

I was born the third child in a family of six, in Dundalk, Ontario, where everyone knew everyone else's business. By the time I was three, my parents suspected I was Deaf and took me to Sick Children's Hospital in Toronto where it was confirmed. Although they tried to provide for me at home, by the time I was five, my parents knew I needed to be part of the larger Deaf community.

I attended the Residential School for the Deaf in Belleville and still maintain contact with friends I met that year. Because the school was over capacity with 600 to 700 students on the same campus – imagine the thriving community with all those Deaf kids – I was eventually transferred to the new school for the Deaf in Milton. I graduated in 1971. I loved school life! I was so fortunate and have lots of really good memories from those days, but that would take another book to describe.

I attended Gallaudet University for a short time but I did not see any point in staying there. I wanted to be a teacher and at that time Ontario schools would not even think of hiring Deaf teachers. There was also the little matter of the boyfriend, so I came home. I think it was a blessing in disguise because I got to know my Dad more before he passed away.

I met Jim just before I graduated from Milton School for the Deaf. Our wedding was something else. We asked Reverend Bob Rumball from Bob Rumball Centre for the Deaf in Toronto to wed us at the Calvary United Church in St. Jacobs where our pastor had never heard a minister who could sign. He was so impressed with Reverend Bob Rumball that each year on Palm Sunday he still invites Reverend Rumball to give a sermon with all proceeds to go towards the Centre.

Jim and I have two wonderful hearing children, Jason, 20 and Jeri, 17, and two cats. We had an afghan hound dog named Deafy who passed away. She was unique in that she would run to the door when she saw the light flashing. She would watch us in sign language and when we said, "Let's give some leftovers to Deafy" she would come up. She knew to bark if my kids were around but would come up to me to get attention.

I am now working as a Project Director for the Canadian Deaf Heritage project under the auspices of the Canadian Cultural Society of the Deaf. Our mandate is to expand American Sign Language Literature and Deaf Literature across Canada, produce an American Sign Language and English children's literature videotape series, broadcast productions with TVOntario and advocate for progress in literacy at all levels of the education of Deaf children. We have also initiated the Ladder Awards™ program to celebrate stories within Deaf culture and to increase the small amount of published Canadian ASL literature and Deaf literature that exists today.

All my life I have wanted people to enjoy and celebrate life the way it should be and this book is the next step in this journey. My desire to write this book started when we had our children, both of whom are hearing. We were able to see the differences they experienced in school and the experiences of our niece and nephew, both of whom are Deaf. What I began to realize was that, despite various laws designed to protect the rights of children in general, Deaf children are often excluded, misinterpreted or ignored. Perhaps this book will help parents understand that they are not alone in their challenge of raising a Deaf child. I want them to really know their Deaf child and what he or she needs – basic human rights.

Each child is a unique person with a right to be heard. This right is particularly significant for Deaf children because they can easily be ignored or overlooked. Again and again, in my encounters with Deaf children, the same issues and conflicts assert themselves. In this book I hope to explain several of these problems and suggest what can be done to alleviate or solve them.

This book is intended to help parents and other people learn more about Deaf children by using Deaf adults, who were once Deaf children, as resources. The stories on the following pages are actual experiences that have not been included in research studies. My approach is admittedly personal and anecdotal. I concentrate on real-life experiences rather than so-called hard data largely because we in the Deaf community are living examples of the problems outlined in this book. Much of the information currently available on Deaf issues is well intentioned but biased simply because it reflects the attitudes and assumptions of those in the hearing world – researchers, teachers, speech and language pathologists, doctors, etc. By taking a more personal approach, I hope to encourage others who are Deaf to relate their own experiences and, in so doing, gain the solidarity needed to solve the problems that confront us all.

In the chapters that follow, it may seem that I am unduly critical of people in the hearing community, but my real aim is understanding, not blame. Let me explain my perspective with a short anecdote I call the Squirrel Analogy. One day when I came home, my thirteen-year-old daughter ran up to me, quite upset and anxious. She explained that a squirrel had been coming up to the bird feeder attached to our window, trying to eat some peanuts. Certain that something was wrong, she said, "the squirrel has no fur from the waist down and is so skinny. We've got to do something to help it."

Not being an expert on squirrels but not wanting to admit it, I explained what we could do to help poor, sick animals. Then I remembered that my daughter's grandmother knew a lot about squirrels. So I told her to phone her grandma and ask for advice. After a lengthy conversation on the phone, my daughter hung up, her face lit with excitement. She explained, "Grandma said that the squirrel was not sick and that we shouldn't do any of the things that we talked about doing. The squirrel has babies in our backyard! Grandma says she has no fur from the waist down because she is making a nest out of her fur for her babies. She is very hungry and we can help by giving her peanut butter sandwiches."

The point of the analogy is this: we should not jump to conclusions based on our own assumptions. We first need to get the whole picture and find the experts who can fit the pieces of the puzzle together. If we try to interfere with nature just because we think there is a need, we could end up doing more harm than good. The same lesson applies to the situation of Deaf children. We often try to "fix" the child according to hearing standards because we assume that this is what they need and want. Instead, we must do our best to see things from the perspective of the Deaf child and, more importantly, to protect his or her rights. By doing so, we can help that child attain genuine independence and self-reliance.

ADVOCACY FOR YOUR DEAF CHILD

Every Deaf child has the right:

- to preserve his or her natural rights;
- to have full access to communication and information;
- to participate in cultural activities which are on par with those of hearing children;
- to choose from a full range of educational opportunities;
- to develop his or her full potential both as an individual and as a contributing member of the community; and
- to receive the opportunity to contribute and to help build a prosperous, responsible society.

In other words, every Deaf child has the right to belong.

INTRODUCTION

Quiet Journey

Butterflies, you made me look
Up from the flower I almost took.
I see your shower of silent wings.
Through the meadow silence sings.
Can anyone so quiet be
And yet gleam so brilliantly?

Marion Marlene Stephens
Poetry to Greet the Heart II

BEING DEAF is a way of life for me. I come from a family of eight, seven of whom are hearing. My husband is Deaf and our two teenagers are hearing. I consider myself culturally Deaf, meaning that I am a member of the Deaf community using American Sign Language (ASL) not only as my primary language but also as my preferred language.

When I was growing up, my family was good, hardworking, intelligent and loving. They did the best they could for me considering the lack of resources available to them at that time, but it was hard.

According to Mom's account of my early years, there

were times when I would be sitting up in my crib after a nap, not noticing her come into the room until I saw her in the mirror over the dresser. At one, I was walking and saying the odd word, but by two, my mother suspected something was wrong with my hearing. When I was three, I had trouble with my ears. My temperature would rise to 103 or 104° F during the night. When the doctor checked me the next day, he found nothing wrong. In June of that year, while we were living at Elliot Lake, Mom made an appointment for me at the Hospital for Sick Children in Toronto. I was prescribed mycilin capsules to fight strep infection. At that time, Mom was sure I could hear. When she called me, I would turn; when she asked me for a kleenex, I would get her one. She almost cancelled the appointment, her third one, but then I became Deaf again. At the hospital, Dr. Prichard examined me from head to toe and found that I was "intelligent" and "deaf." I was referred to Dr. Strattan who recommended I attend the Deaf Residential School at Belleville (now the Sir James Whitney School for the Deaf). To this day, I sure am glad he made that recommendation, even though it was four hundred miles from where we lived.

My parents had limited experience and information and there was a lack of resources available. They did not have much money, but much planning went into the long trip to Belleville. My dad made a trailer and bought a used tent. Everything was packed into the trailer to be hauled behind the old car. I knew what was going on. We had already visited schools in Sudbury and Ottawa where I had looked around and shook my head, "No." When we got to the school in Belleville I nodded, "Yes." We camped at Trenton Park the first night. We were rained out that night and the next. My mom and dad secured the old tent to the top of the homemade trailer. It was a strange sight!

Luckily only one other group was there to see us. I was so happy I was going to go to school in Belleville. I was almost six years old.

My parents wished they had learned ASL for me. My mom wrote in her journal, "I have regretted not learning sign language, but my memory now keeps me busy to remember even one language. Someday, somewhere, I hope [Joanne] has forgiven us. It would have made life so much easier for her."

My mother's letters to me at school revealed the heart of a woman who was trying desperately to do what the medical and educational experts thought was best for her child. My dad wrote to me as well and one of my teachers commented on how few of the dads put forth so much effort. I have obviously benefited by having the loving support of my family behind me; perhaps I could have communicated my love for them better if they had known sign language.

I attended two provincial schools for the Deaf, the Sir James Whitney School for the Deaf in Belleville and the E. C. Drury School for the Deaf in Milton. This was where I was first exposed to Deaf culture and learned ASL, a new experience for me which I still cherish to this day.

Getting an education, particularly a higher education, has been an ongoing struggle because of the lack of communication interaction with my environment. When I graduated from high school I went to Lougheed Business College in Kitchener where I had to make do with partial information, thus receiving a partial education. A girl sitting next to me in class decided to take notes for me. It was not a struggle to pass the course but it was not smooth sailing either. Using interpreters on and off, I attended the University of Waterloo and various colleges. Only at Gallaudet University in the United States, however, did I experience a full signing environment (that is, ASL).

Joanne S. Cripps

My experiences at the University of Waterloo were exasperating. I took one course for which I needed course notes. I was given the transcripts but I had to pay for them. An auxiliary woman helped me pay and they refused to give me credit for the course until I had paid in full for the transcripts. I also had a struggle to find funding for the interpreter once I had found one. I encountered similar communication barriers in the working world

Over the years, one of my chief frustrations has been that, even though I felt I had the intellectual potential and leadership skills to take on more responsible positions, I lacked the opportunity to put these qualities to good use. Fortunately, I had a role model who made a huge difference in my life. One of the first Deaf teachers to work at a Deaf residential school, Anne McKercher, encouraged me to apply there for the position of a residential counsellor. I was granted an interview, which I attended without an interpreter. Using my voice, I answered questions well enough, apparently, to get the job. A few years later, we lobbied to get interpreter services, ASL and Deaf Culture incorporated into the school, eventually launching a pilot project called Bilingual-Bicultural Deaf Education.

For over eighteen years, I have taught ASL to hearing adults as well as English as a Second Language (ESL) to Deaf adults. My first teaching experience was to a group of 50 Mennonite people who wanted to learn ASL and the cultural need for it, for the Deaf children in their community. Even though I was pregnant, had no sign language resources and had to develop my own sign language lesson plans, I was amazed to discover how many people wanted to learn how to sign.

I represented the Canadian Cultural Society of the Deaf at the Bilingual-Bicultural Deaf Education conference in Sweden in 1993. This was an enlightening experience for me as I realized there are similar goals and barriers throughout the world for Deaf people. We all need to work together.

When I worked as an advocate, I was not allowed to suggest to parents that they obtain and use closed caption decoders for televisions as this would have been considered political motivation: I would have been promoting Deaf culture. There are many agencies and organizations that benefit from Deaf children learning speech. If I had spoken positively about Deaf culture, this would have indicated that I was choosing sides; that I felt Deaf culture was a more viable way of life than the oral options. If parents believed that not having a closed caption decoder would help children learn lip-reading then I was not to persuade them otherwise. I understood my role and I complied; however, I felt that the parents did not fully comprehend the benefits or the disadvantages of all the options available.

As Project Director of the Canadian Deaf Heritage, I am trying to remove the oppression many Deaf people feel. My responsibilities include: designing training manuals for Deaf/hearing parents with Deaf/hearing children; developing an action plan to expand ASL literature and Deaf literature (English stories with Deaf characters, identity and experience); developing and distributing Deaf heritage information; and, with help from TVOntario, producing ASL and English literature videotapes for children and expanding the ASL literature and Deaf literature awards program known as The Ladder Awards.™

It is my hope that hearing parents will try to expose their Deaf children to a bilingual bicultural Deaf environment. Now that Deaf people are becoming more aware of the need to empower themselves, they have also begun to realize how important it is, not only to educate the public about Deaf rights, but also, to speak out on behalf of all future Deaf children. Understanding their rights means providing each of them with the tools of life, with the ability to reclaim ownership of their lives.

It is understood that food, shelter and communication are basic human rights, but we need to know that Deaf rights must also be observed. Deaf children should be able to lead independent, fulfilling lives just like any child. They should not have to rely on hearing individuals, especially when technology can do the job.

I ask you to take another look at the picture on the cover of this book. The image is one I commissioned Douglas Donald to paint for me. The kids are jumping from the dark past, where there were no rights to sign language and culture, to the bright future. The pickets in the fence depict Deaf rights, illustrated in ASL (from left to right): philosophy, literacy skills, family, love, ownership, learning and remembering, identity, happiness, parents, friends, culture, values, sister, brother, heritage, rights, and a name. On the cobblestone, signs indicate the rights to access, TTY, liberated and independent. The grass shows the freedom to use hands to communicate. By jumping the fence, the kids have acquired a sense of purpose in life.

In discussing rights and privileges, this book makes a significant assumption: it is not appropriate to teach Deaf children the hearing way of doing things as if this is normal. It is inconceivable to have a Deaf child "speak" in front of an audience without first considering his or her feelings and ability to intelligibly speak. It is also inhuman to deny Deaf children access to the Deaf way of doing things. I believe every Deaf person has the right to fulfill their own potential, develop their individual identity and acquire a sense of belonging. Every Deaf person has the right to be Deaf.

CHAPTER ONE

INCLUSION

*All individuals should have an equal opportunity
to make for themselves the lives that they are able
and wish to have, consistent with their duties
and obligations as members of society.*

Canadian Human Rights Act

*I went home that summer anxious to see my family
and show off my new skills. Everyone came to our house to
see a deaf girl speak. Pa asked me to recite "Our Father,"
but I had not practiced it, so I had a hard time. Everyone
looked disappointed. Suddenly, I blurted out the poem
I had recited at school – "Twinkle, Twinkle, Little Star."
The guests started talking and leaving. Pa grinned and
slapped his knee. I was glad I could speak for Pa, but just as
glad I could sign too. I enjoyed being home again,
having fun like before. But I also could not wait to go
back to school where I knew I had many more things to learn.
Best of all, I knew that I could learn everything!*

Christy MacKinnon

Christy MacKinnon (1889 - 1981) was from Nova Scotia. In her book,
Silent Observer, she wrote about her experience going home for the
summer after staying at a Deaf residential school.

INCLUSION

D EAF CHILDREN, like hearing children, see themselves at the centre of their own holistic sphere. When any child starts to develop a sense of how he or she is connected to society, a set of widening circles envelops them. At first, the child is surrounded by family members who love and care for him or her. As time passes, the child becomes more aware of external influences on his or her sphere of reality. Peers begin to have a greater effect. As the child matures, he or she may realize they are part of a minority (religious, ethnic, cultural, etc.) with its own set of including factors. A Deaf child's maturation results in a recognition of his or her part in not only an immediate circle but also as part of a wider social circle, that of the hearing community – the majority of society. Thus inclusion means the Deaf child will ultimately become a contributing member of society.

To experience inclusion a person must feel part of a wider social circle, not isolated or excluded. However, it is important to note that inclusion is viewed in a very specific manner within the Deaf community. For Deaf children, inclusion means: they feel secure, loved, and included in all areas of family life; they have relationships with peers to help gain a knowledge of self; they are provided by the Deaf community with role models, values and a heritage thus ensuring a natural social development within a minority; and they are able to interact with hearing society on a daily basis.

Throughout this book, I refer to Deaf culture and the Deaf community, two terms that require some explanation. Just what is a community? If I am a hearing person, I scarcely have to think of this word's meaning. In a hearing community, I have a school, sports, cultural and social activities, friends and neighbours. By providing the means by which I can engage in these activities and interact with others, my community not only looks after my needs but also develops and reinforces itself.

As a Deaf person, I also need a community to call my own. A Deaf community is a minority culture with shared values and heritage. It is composed of friends and family who have a lot in common and it provides a broad support network to Deaf individuals. Being involved in a Deaf community allows Deaf members to live independently but maintain fellowship with others. If Deaf children are not exposed to the Deaf community they may not develop a strong identity because they will not have a sense of their social ground. (See Chapter Five, Social Ground)

Parents are responsible for supporting their child's language development. In hearing children, this is taken for granted; parents quite naturally support spoken language development by speaking to their child, providing safe opportunities for them to talk to other children and adults, and turning on the radio and television. Deaf children do not get the opportunity to overhear these interactions naturally. Deaf children need to see communication and interaction.

In order to feel included in the family, the Deaf child needs to have a common language with his or her family. By learning American Sign Language (ASL), a visual language, the Deaf child can communicate with parents and other family members who also learn ASL. Agencies such as the Canadian Hearing Society or colleges offer ASL courses at various levels. (See Appendix for more information.) A Deaf mentor or tutor may present a better learning situation for a family with a young Deaf child. Deaf mentors can be found by contacting the local Deaf community. A mentor comes into the home to help foster natural language development in the family while teaching other family members ASL. This situation also provides interaction and links with the Deaf community for both family and child. Qualified Deaf babysitters and caregivers can also help promote ASL while providing role models to Deaf children.

Parents need to be supported in their endeavours to help their child feel included. By learning ASL, they are better able to communicate with their Deaf child. Parents with a Deaf child are provided free of charge a first level ASL course by the Ministry of Education in Ontario if they are enrolled in the Provincial Schools for the Deaf program. This is not enough. Outside Ontario, some classes are provided free of charge or at cost.

Exposing Deaf children to ASL is controversial. Some parents prefer teaching Deaf children spoken English, making use of any residual hearing the child may have. Does this promote inclusion? Do the children get to interact naturally? Will they enjoy their life as much, learn to make mistakes and discuss issues? Does this promote two-way communication? I argue that, although the child may learn to decode the English language, it is not a natural process. English and ASL are two separate languages.

Another way parents can encourage natural language development is to find other Deaf children to play with their child. This also develops necessary social skills. Peers are an important part of social development. Like all children, Deaf children need to have friends with the same interests. They need to make friends, play sports and interact with others. In order to do this, there must be a shared language base so inner and outer conflicts can be identified and solved. Deaf peers provide the necessary social interaction to help the Deaf child become aware of him or herself.

Associations and organizations such as the Canadian Association of the Deaf, Canadian Deaf Sports Association and the Canadian Cultural Society of the Deaf may be able to provide information about local Deaf communities, Deaf camps and Deaf events. Information can also be found from the Deaf Network sources on the Internet. Deaf schools can be contacted to learn about preschool programs. See the Appendix for more resource information.

A Deaf child's natural social development also requires exposure to Deaf language and culture in the Deaf community through social events, activities and sports. Knowledge of the Deaf community is essential through school years. Deaf schools provide a residential setting in which students may live in residences at the school, allowing for constant interaction with Deaf role models who are already in the Deaf community. This is not to say students must live in residence; these resources are simply components of the community. When hearing students graduate from secondary school, they have developed a network of contacts. As the Deaf child matures and graduates from secondary school, he or she will know who to contact if he or she wants to be involved in the Deaf community.

Hearing administrators and teachers in schools very often do not know what is going on in the Deaf world; hence, they lack knowledge that could reinforce Deaf culture in proper curriculum design. They may know that Deaf culture is out there, but may feel it is not necessary to find out what is happening and what the current issues are. Hearing parents may also be unaware of events in the Deaf community; of course, it is not their fault. Everyone in contact with the Deaf child should have an understanding of the Deaf world. For example, teachers cannot just teach a Deaf child one aspect of education and then go home thinking his or her job is done. Teachers, residential counsellors and parents can all learn more about the Deaf world by surfing the Internet, reading newspapers and just being aware of the people and events around them.

As a Deaf adult, I am very involved in the hearing community; however, my role in hearing culture is not my whole life. My two children are hearing and I need to expose them to the world in which they are growing up. My husband and I nurture their environment by making sure they get a lot of "sound" stimulus. At the same time, we expose them to, and share with them, our Deaf language and culture. We do not say, "I am sorry but this is my language. You must fit in with our system." Instead we share with them what we have. We have the radio and television on every day for spoken language exposure. Our children also have constant contact with the hearing members of our family. This helps them acquire their own identity in the family structure. We use ASL in the home as well as a teletypewriter (TTY) and a voice telephone that allow for the private exchange of information.

Deaf people are constantly involved in hearing society. Without language access, the Deaf can be isolated from the rest of society. Some people believe that inclusion means simply providing support services to meet the information translation needs of the Deaf, but interpreters do not replace natural social development. True inclusion means much more than giving Deaf children access to the hearing world through instruction in sign language. Inclusion should allow full participation in all aspects of life. Deaf children should be able to feel self-confident with friends and part of a community of their own, so they can become contributing members of society.

It seems redundant to say that a child needs to feel included in his or her own family for how could children not feel included in their own family? But in fact, clear communication, which provides children with the opportunity to express themselves, understand one another and participate in discussions about issues that involve them, is restricted for Deaf children. Learning only takes place when ideas are shared. Morals and values are passed from generation to generation through language.

How can parents help Deaf children feel included?

• Provide a safe and secure environment in which to learn. Use visible communication, be it writing or signing. Make sure all members of the family can communicate using this language. Keep in mind that a naturally acquired language is easier for any child to learn.

• Provide opportunities for your Deaf child to participate equally in family life. A flashing light, indicating a ringing doorbell, fire alarm or telephone, allows the Deaf child to have equal access to what is happening in the home. A vibrating or flashing light alarm clock allows the Deaf child to be more independent. Closed-caption television decoders transcribe many shows, allowing Deaf children to understand the programs and news on television.

• Involve your Deaf child with his or her peers. Playgroups are not only good for children, but also for parents. Deaf day camps are available in many major cities across Canada; some of these also offer positions for siblings who are hearing. There are also camps run outside large cities where Deaf children can stay overnight. Other opportunities where children can interact include Deaf Children's Festivals, held throughout Canada, and each province has a Cultural Society of the Deaf that organizes an annual or biennial festival for Deaf children in schools.

• Learn about events that are occurring in the Deaf world. Where will the next Deaf Olympic Games be held? Are there any Deaf athletes living in the same area as your child? Learn about famous Deaf Canadian athletes. For example, Ottawa runner Paul Landry is one of Canada's top male competitors in middle and long distance running. He ran in national and provincial championships for ten years and represented Canada five times at the World Summer Games for the Deaf. Ottawa has named a local park in his honour. Joanne Robinson from British Columbia was considered the best all-around Deaf female swimmer in the world. In 1967, at the 11th World Summer Games for the Deaf in Yugoslavia, she broke her own 1965 world record in the 100-metre freestyle.

- Expose your Deaf child to everything. Let your child play instruments and feel music – experiment with drums, do Deaf raps, strum a guitar or tickle the ivories on a piano. Allow your child to order at a restaurant by showing the waiter what he or she wants using a pen and paper or gestures. Children should also be allowed to pay for their own purchases at stores. Allow them to interact with the hearing society as all children do. They will learn to be independent.

Chapter Two

Access to Communication

*Knowledge is the eye of desire
and can become the pilot of the soul.*

Will Durant

ACCESS TO COMMUNICATION

ONE DAY my eight-year-old hearing daughter was sitting at the kitchen table, watching and listening intently as my mother and I communicated using Deaf speech and a bit of writing. She suddenly stopped us and asked, "Grandma, how did you talk to my mom when she was little?"

Unsure of what to say, my mother finally replied, "Well, I taught Joanne to talk and now she can talk."

"Yes, I know," my daughter said. "But how did you *communicate* with my mom?"

I find it amazing that my daughter seemed to know instinctively how important a natural language really is. To her, what my mother and I were doing must have appeared artificial and that, in her eyes, ASL seemed to be my natural language.

I do not hold my mother responsible for the fact that she didn't learn ASL. Given the chance, I believe she would have learned sign language but, at that time, teaching ASL was considered inappropriate – almost taboo. Virtually no resources were made available to those who wanted to learn ASL.

13

During my years at the residential school for Deaf children, I was taught how to speak. It seemed that the focus was on learning speech, not on education. I felt as if I was trying to communicate in a foreign language. I remember being in a play for the Open House. They made me speak in front of the audience. It was nerve-racking. I worried about how I sounded. Does my voice sound nice? Clear? Does it grate?

Deaf students who excelled in using their voices were deemed "successes." The teachers felt these students had worked hard to achieve this and deserved praise. Parents applauded them; it was so wonderful for these students to be able to "talk." I felt like a dog in training. I had questions about my schoolwork but I didn't know who to ask or how, even though I won the Best Speech and Language Award.

One year, after my return home for summer vacation, I went to an army base airport to look at planes with my family. My dad was taking pictures. I yelled, "Daddy to stop." My mom started to cry because I spoke the three words perfectly. But ironically, I said those words because I was trained to say them, not because I understood their meaning.

At that time, the required communication method for Deaf students was oral speech. I did not have expressive oral skills, even though I understood. It was one-way communication. My concerns were not addressed; my frustrations not recognized. I could not communicate my thoughts and feelings in a way that others could understand. If sign language had been part of my upbringing, my childhood would have been a happier time.

Communication allows people to make their needs known to others. They can express feelings, thoughts and abstract ideas, as well as understand what others are conveying. Communication is easy when people converse in the same language. It is difficult, however, when two people with different languages try to "talk" with each other. This is the case when a Deaf person and a hearing person speak.

Freire and Macedo (1987) identified three levels of literacy: functional, cultural and critical literacy. Functional literacy is the technical mastery of particular skills necessary to decode simple texts such as street signs, instruction manuals or the front page of the newspaper. Cultural literacy involves being familiar with particular linguistic traditions or bodies of information and acquiring a knowledge of selected works of literature and historical information necessary for informed participation in the political and cultural life of a particular society. Critical literacy is the ability to decode the ideological dimensions of texts, institutions, social practices and cultural forms such as television and film in order to reveal their selective interests. It involves being able to analyze and challenge oppressive characteristics of a society so that a more just, equitable and democratic society can be created.

It is important to stress the fact that American Sign Language (ASL) is not a "communication method." ASL is a language in which people interact much the same as they would in a spoken language. For Deaf individuals, interacting using ASL is as natural as breathing. It is a way of life. For a Deaf person in a distinctive Deaf culture, ASL is the communication link with others; it has its own syntax, grammar and morphology, as many prominent researchers will testify.

ASL is a beautifully expressive, visual language that allows for communication on all levels – metaphorical, formal, colloquial – just as any other language does. ASL allows Deaf people to communicate without barriers. It is easily accessible, naturally acquired and expressed through visible signs and gestures. It is learned in the same manner as a spoken language – incidentally and instinctively.

I was first exposed to ASL by a Deaf girl, Helen Wojcik, whose parents were Deaf. I was six years old. It was my first year at the Deaf Residential School. We did not learn ASL in class. As a matter of fact, we were not allowed to sign in school or at mealtimes in the residence. Students who were caught signing were punished. Unlike me, Helen always seemed to know what was going on around her – she was an active participant in her own life. It was Helen who bravely taught all her friends how to sign and finger-spell when the teachers were not looking.

Before I started learning signs I felt out of the picture. I felt that I was not a participant in life but rather a disconnected observer watching the world from behind a glass wall. I could see my sisters arguing and laughing and talking at the dinner table, but I was never a part of that. When I first went to residential school, I was not sure how I would fit in with the students there either. I felt wary of the others; they seemed to know what they were doing and where they were going while I didn't.

When Helen taught us ASL, I don't think she felt as though she were teaching a language. She just knew how to interact using a visual language because her Deaf parents had taught her. She was surprised that the counsellors in residence could not sign.

Helen was a great storyteller. Oh, the stories she could tell us! We loved it. We laughed. We cried. We complained. We begged for more stories. Sometimes Helen would tease us: "If I tell you a story, what will you give me?" It was clear that she enjoyed telling us stories because she felt she was sharing something with us that we ought to have.

I felt empowered when I learned ASL. It was a strange feeling to know I could receive information and also give information back. At first, it felt like I had learned something forbidden. When the students went downtown or to church, we would lower our hands to sign, communicating amongst ourselves in our own little world. We felt proud of the fact that we knew how to do this and no one else did. We would sit in circles outside, swarming around Helen, and "whisper" – our heads lowered as we shared the secrets of the world outside us.

As people from other cultures have a mother tongue, so do Deaf people – ASL. That does not mean that ASL is the only viable language for Deaf people or that it must be adhered to throughout eternity. Many people use more than one language proficiently. Deaf people are no different. They may also want to learn English, French or other languages. After proficiently acquiring a first language, it is much easier to understand and be efficient in the grammar and mechanics of a second and third and fourth language.

Although it is my opinion that ASL is a natural language base for Deaf people, using it with their child is an issue that parents must think about. Hearing parents of Deaf children will most likely not have the means or the knowledge to teach ASL to their children. When they realize that their child is Deaf, they look for information on how to help their child communicate. Most often this search begins in a doctor's office where many options are presented involving medical intervention. (See Chapter Seven, Access to Information.) Very little information is imparted about Deaf culture, meeting Deaf people and learning ASL, because these are not considered medically helpful to the child. Parents must look to external organizations to find more information at a time when they might still be in the process of grieving that their child has a "hearing impairment." They frequently do not know where to look.

When discussing communication, parents need to know that only one option – the use of ASL – provides a fully accessible language for Deaf children. In fact, I would suggest that it really is not an option at all, but rather an imperative. I believe that all the other options are limited and do not provide the opportunities they may initially seem to.

We all know that a child learns a lot from the environment. When my two hearing children were born, we knew right away what they needed: a sound environment, opportunities to interact with people who speak, a hearing school, sports and music. Deaf parents with Deaf children know right away what environment their children need too: a visual environment with closed-captioned programs on TV; opportunities to interact with both Deaf and hearing ASL users; a TTY; interaction with Deaf role models and Deaf peers; Deaf schools or schools with a large Deaf population; and sports, music and other cultural events.

Now, let's focus on the situation of a Deaf child of hearing parents and help these parents understand the environment their Deaf child will need.

Social programs must be in place and available to all Deaf students. Sports programs, either after school or after supper, are valuable experiences. Residential schools have an increasing number of Deaf teachers and Deaf professionals who provide excellent role models for their students. If a Deaf student chooses an ASL program, then there are more chances that the student will be at a residential school; thus, sports are more easily accessible. All children need social interaction. Most children go to community programs after school, but Deaf children are restricted because of communication barriers and problems they encounter with their Deaf identity. Parents should tell, not ask, schools to include their Deaf children in their extracurricular activities. Such activities can include an ASL storytelling series, house league sports and social/individual activities such as table games tournaments. We must advocate to include these programs because they are the school's responsibilities; they help develop literacy skills. Make life even more exciting for your Deaf child by encouraging activities after school or after supper; otherwise, it will be just school, bus and home, perhaps eating potato chips in front of the TV.

The thought of growing up in a hearing society that is silently, unintentionally oppressive makes me feel anxious. The hearing community appears to value highly the oral method of communication – speech and hearing. To communicate with hearing individuals, and thus the rest of the world, it appears that Deaf people need to speak. People claiming that they want to help "normalize" Deaf individuals give the message that to be normal you must be able to speak. Little regard was given – and this continues today – to the fact that Deaf people already have a strong communication system. This may not be a conscious intent; however, it affects Deaf individuals in that it marginalizes our natural communication.

Deaf people who use ASL as their language of communication can interact with the hearing society without speaking. Written communication has been used for years to convey the needs and wants of Deaf people – ordering in restaurants, conducting banking transactions and dealing with doctors can be done easily in writing. Often, in this age of technology, people do not even need to communicate face-to-face: personal and professional business can be conducted through e-mail and the Internet. In addition, a telephone relay service can connect Deaf people with the hearing society using a teletype machine (TTY) to type a message which is then read by a relay service operator to the hearing person on the other end. Many major organizations now have their own TTY, hence, calls can be made directly to hearing businesses, hospitals, government offices and other destinations. ASL interpreters can also be used to translate in situations that need longer and more detailed explanations.

Deaf people have fought long and hard for their rights to be recognized. Ontario, the first province in Canada to go beyond English and French, now recognizes ASL and LSQ (*Langue des Signes Québécois*) as official languages of instruction (Section 11, Bill 4). This Bill was the product of an organized movement by the Ontario Association of the Deaf's (OAD) Education Task Force. Beginning in 1988, the OAD lobbied the government to recognize Deaf people as part of a distinct culture. The struggle took five long years of legislative delays and a change in government but finally Bill 4 was passed.

Incredibly enough, despite the increased recognition of Deaf realities that has developed in the last decade or so, many problems persist. For example, even though the right to use our natural sign language is slowly being recognized by society at large, we must still overcome the idea that it is an optional method of language learning. The misuse of the phrase "ASL-trained children" shows that a change in awareness is still very much needed. ASL is not a method of training. It is a distinct language that cannot be artificially taught to Deaf children; rather, it is their natural language, acquired by interaction with their peers and their environment.

I recommend that parents of Deaf children who learn ASL will find it is the best way to communicate. The

Quiet Journey

whole family will need to communicate throughout the child's life and it is a joy to be able to communicate directly with your Deaf child, to discuss many different things. The extra time you spend communicating will be beneficial in many ways. It will allow you to be involved in every aspect of your child's life. It will help develop your relationship. Communicating together will expand your child's repertoire of language and it will show your Deaf child that you value the person that he or she is regardless of the language he or she uses.

CHAPTER THREE

IDENTITY

Proud to be Deaf

Being Deaf is one of my best qualities,
It's helped me become aware of all minorities,
To broaden my mind,
To understand the difference between
Prejudice and Discrimination.
Being Deaf has allowed me to talk and sing
In a beautiful language that is visual.
Being Deaf has given me the opportunity
To experience life in a dorm along with my peers.
It has taught me to be independent and to never give up.
I learned that there are a variety of ways to communicate,
There are no limitations so I never limit myself.
Being Deaf has put me through hard times
And I have learned several things the hard way.
Being Deaf has allowed me to live in two different worlds
And to communicate with others
whose language differs from mine.
Being Deaf has made me a stronger person,
It has allowed me to find the true meaning of pride.
Being Deaf has made me the person I am today
And I am proud of who I am,
No doubt about it!

Aimee Whyte

Aimee is enrolled in her fourth year at the Rochester Institute of Technology College with a major in Professional and Technical Communications. Born Deaf to Deaf parents, she has a younger sister who is also Deaf. Aimee has been writing poetry since the age of ten. In her own words, "Through poetry, I am able to express my innermost thoughts, feelings and experiences. Being Deaf is part of my whole life." It is interesting and relevant to consider if poetry either in written form or in ASL composed by Deaf individuals has a very different function from poetry composed by hearing individuals. As with any language, each would have their own definition and structure of poetry. The different styles of interpretation displayed in Deaf poetry show how we as Deaf poets assemble our thoughts and experiences very differently from hearing poets.

IDENTITY

ONE OF THE MOST important learning experiences in my life happened at a workshop at the Ontario Institute for Studies in Education in the early 1970s. Dr. Roy Holcombe was the guest speaker. He opened his presentation by walking up to the stage and speaking inaudibly. People in the audience leaned forward to hear what he was saying but could not understand a word. Then an ASL interpreter came on stage and Dr. Holcombe began to speak clearly. He told the audience that this type of experience is what Deaf people go through trying to access full information. Prior to this eye-opening experience, I never felt Deaf people had the right to have an ASL interpreter for workshops. From then on, I never looked back.

Another triumph happened about seven years ago. My sister, Mossie, who was working and living in Calgary at that time, called me via the Message Relay Service. She announced she was going to quit her job and attend the ASL Interpreting Training program at Sheridan College. I was very surprised. My first thoughts were, "What would my friends say about her signing skills? Why hadn't she learned ASL when we were kids? What will it be like to have someone in the family who can sign?" It had been my lifelong wish, but to have this goal announced threw me off guard.

Mossie entered the program and stayed at our place for six months so she could be exposed to ASL in a Deaf environment and to Deaf culture generally. She saw me in my natural element, which she hadn't seen before. My kids, who are hearing, were unsure of their role. Should they sign and speak to her at the same time? They felt responsible because Mossie didn't always understand ASL. When we felt we were losing ground, I banged on the table and said to them, "Look, Mossie came here to learn ASL, so we will use ASL at this table."

Mossie was surprised to discover the other side of the world we live in. I learned more family gossip than I felt I had a right to. At times, I felt it was too much. I was not used to having someone in the family who could sign. When Mossie became more fluent in ASL, we started to enjoy her company more and more. It was beautiful. I am glad to have this opportunity now, despite the years it took us to reach it. We both broke through the glass wall – each learning more about the other and the lives we've chosen to live.

When we think about identity, we think about who we are now, where we have come from, and what factors have influenced our values and decisions. Article 8 of the United Nations Convention on the Rights of the Child focuses on the preservation of identity. It states, "Parties undertake to respect the right of the child to preserve his or her identity, including nationality, name and family relations as recognized by law without unlawful interference." The question is, how can Deaf children be afforded this same right?

From a very early age, all children need to have an identity. All of us are aware of the symbolic, personal and social significance of our names, our given names in particular. From the time they are babies, children love to hear and see their name being used. It helps them to feel loved and know their place in the world.

It is a parent's responsibility to nurture and care for his or her child, allowing the child to develop emotionally, socially and physically. A strong sense of self promotes confidence and self-esteem. By using the child's name constantly, parents encourage emotional growth.

Names are just as important to a Deaf child and his or her identity but there are cultural differences in the naming process. Most children of Deaf parents receive a name sign at birth; Deaf children born to hearing parents are also given name signs, usually when they start residential school or when the Deaf child first meets other ASL-using Deaf individuals.

For example, when I first started attending residential school I was given a name sign by Deaf girls who were in the senior residence. They observed all of the junior girls carefully and then named us. A name sign is usually indicated by signing one initial in the person's name on a particular spot on the face, head or upper body, or in a neutral space in front of the upper body. Each letter of the alphabet has a handshape. In my case, a "J" handshape was used on the cheek in a motion to indicate my dimples.

In his book *The Book of Name Signs: Naming in American Sign Language*, Samuel J. Supalla discusses in detail the naming process for Deaf individuals. There are some differences between Canada and the United States, but research is just now starting north of the border. According to Supalla, there are two different systems of name signs: descriptive and arbitrary. Descriptive name signs have a meaning, such as the name sign described above given to me when I was young, but an arbitrary name sign does not refer to any physical attributes or personal characteristics.

The natural process of giving name signs was altered during the period when a system known as Signed English became prevalent in the schools. After a period of teaching Deaf students orally/aurally, signing began to be allowed. However, the signing was in English word order and there were invented signs to indicate articles, pronouns and pluralization. Hearing people who taught Signed English explained that name signs were given based on a person's personality or recognizable features, e.g. long, curly hair.

Historically name signs were given by a Deaf person who also had a Deaf family. He or she understood the conventions, rules and values inherent in Deaf culture. At that time, name signs were common. For example, the name Linda would be indicated by an "L" handshape tapped twice on the opposite front of the shoulder. If there were two Lindas, the second one would have either her surname initial or any recognizable feature sign added to her common name sign.

We need to educate those who unintentionally use demeaning labels to identify the Deaf and hard-of-hearing population. Even now, some people still use the phrase "Deaf and dumb" or "Deaf mute." Technically, in this case, the word dumb means "unable to speak", but to most people, and to Deaf people in particular, this word means "stupid." Similarly, if Deaf children sometimes choose not to use their voice, they should not be considered mute. To be labeled either dumb or mute can be insulting. Unfortunately, the euphemisms used as alternatives can also be offensive. Although terms like "special," "exceptional" or "hearing-impaired" are meant to imply positive attributes and to prevent discrimination, they sometimes have the opposite effect. Too often there is a strong connotation of inferiority in such words and phrases. We label such children because they are different, but we often forget the one thing that we have in common – our humanity. We have no trouble thinking about hearing children as unique individuals with different potentials; we need to accord the same right to Deaf children. They are just Deaf.

If we don't start educating others about these issues, attitudes are not likely to change. Perhaps we can start with our own relatives, even favourite aunts, uncles and cousins who must be made aware of how important names are to Deaf children's sense of identity. Deaf children, especially within the family, have a right to be known by name. Not that long ago, one of my sisters was visiting my uncle. They began to talk about family members, especially another sister who was learning ASL. Upon hearing this fact, my uncle said, "It's good that your sister is learning ASL to help her Deaf and dumb sister." My sister did not correct him. "Well, you know," she later said to me, "some people are like that. They don't mean any harm."

Maybe so, but people who don't mean any harm can still unintentionally hurt others. I advised my sister that, since she knew such terms were offensive, she was obliged to correct him. All of us have the same obligation. Those who mean no harm will probably take no offense.

There is more to this issue than individual identity; there is also the identity that comes from recognizing Deaf children's place in family history. Because communication is easier, hearing children often receive more information about their relatives than their Deaf siblings do. Shouldn't Deaf children have equal access to such information, especially when we consider how hungry they may be for details of their family tree? If communication is a barrier, then using an interpreter from time to time would be a good solution. Taking the Deaf child out to dinner, along with the interpreter, of course, could be a special occasion to satisfy this natural curiosity about his or her family tree.

How can parents help foster a strong sense of identity in their Deaf children?

- Allow your Deaf child to interact and social-ize with other Deaf children.

- Invite Deaf friends into the home so the chil-dren can feel connected with Deaf culture.

- Interaction within the Deaf community will allow the natural process of naming to occur. Until a name sign has been given, parents and relatives should finger-spell the child's name.

- Find out about preschool programs in your area. Deaf residential schools can provide home visiting programs for preschoolers. They can be a good contact for finding other preschoolers in the area.

- If your teenager has not been exposed to Deaf culture or ASL, do not despair. Take the oppor-tunity now to allow the teenager to learn about a culture and language that could be part of his or her life in the future.

- Share family history with your Deaf child, allowing him or her to feel a part of the strong structure of the family. If language seems to slow the process down, do not be afraid to seek the help of interpreters, mentors or friends. Your child needs to be aware of his or her family history. Keep scrapbooks and share personal anecdotes. Allow children to be involved in family gossip and secrets.

• Find out if you have any Deaf relatives and make an effort to make their acquaintance.

CHAPTER FOUR

LANGUAGE AND CULTURE

We Deaf

We laugh when we're happy.
We cry when we're upset.
We cheer when we win.
We scream when we're scared.
We yell for fun.
We shout when we're angry.
We make noises.
Why do you call us silent?
Tell me why.

Janis Cripps, 14

Janis is partially Deaf and comes from a Deaf family. She wrote this poem because she wanted to inform those who think that Deaf persons are quiet and never noisy that they are wrong. In her words, "we do have voices and we know how to express ourselves through laughing, crying and so on." When she wrote this poem, she felt that Deaf people were not being heard enough.

LANGUAGE AND CULTURE

ARTICLES 29 AND 30 of the UN Convention on the Rights of the Child speak to the importance of language and culture in all children's lives. Article 29 1(c) states, "Parties agree that the education of the child shall be directed to the development of respect for the child's parents, his or her own cultural identity, language and values, for the national values of the country in which the child is living, the country from which he or she may originate, and for civilizations different from his or her own."

The UN Convention was developed with all ethnic and national languages and cultures in mind. I submit that it needs to be extended to ensure that Deaf culture has the same rights applied to its linguistic and cultural minority. A hearing person from an ethnic minority background living in Canada is able to interact freely with members of both his or her own cultural identity and the country in which he or she resides. A Deaf child who is without Deaf community contact is analogous to a hearing person from an ethnic minority living within a majority culture with no contact with his or her country of origin, tradition,

JOANNE S. CRIPPS

language, values and cultural identity. Language and culture go hand in hand. Without a common language, people within a community cannot share beliefs, values and traditions. Deaf children also have the right to know about the culture to which they have a birthright. But to be able to understand and partake in Deaf culture, the Deaf child must first have access to clear communication. Without knowing and using ASL, the Deaf child cannot have a full understanding of Deaf culture.

Dr. Laura Ann Petitto, a well-known professor of psychology at McGill University, is interested in how people acquire language as well as how language is organized in the brain. Her research shows that, "Deaf children exposed to signed languages from birth acquire these languages on an identical maturational time course as hearing children acquire spoken languages. They do so without any modification, loss or delay to the timing, content and maturational course associated with reaching all linguistic milestones observed in spoken language." (Petitto, 1999)

If a child chooses to join the Deaf community, he or she may, as indicated in the previous chapter, be involved in two cultures. The child may be acquiring a primary language and learning another language, both of which need to be developed. The Deaf child has the same right to learn both English and ASL as any other minority child who learns their heritage (i.e., minority) language as well as a language spoken throughout the country. Article 30 of the United Nations Convention on the Rights of the Child states clearly, "In those states in which ethnic, religious or linguistic minorities or persons of indigenous origin exist, a child belonging to such a minority or who is indigenous shall not be denied the right, in community with other members of his or her group, to enjoy his or her own culture, to profess and practice his or her own religion, or to use his or her own language." The Deaf child has a Deaf community and a distinct language only if he or she is exposed to both.

Deaf culture is easy to explain by comparing it with other cultures which involve groups sharing common beliefs, values and ethics, using a common language which allows communication among its members at all levels (colloquial, formal, etc.).

So what is unique about Deaf culture? As with any culture, it would take another book to explain it all, but there are a few things that that may help readers understand the "feel" of Deaf culture.

Although Deaf people have varying degrees of hearing, it is common for a Deaf person's other senses (sight, smell, taste, touch) to be enhanced. Deaf children use a lot of visual cues, whereas hearing children rely on both visual and oral cues. For example, when a Deaf person wants the attention of another Deaf person who is sitting at the other end of a cafeteria table he or she will wave with a downward motion of the hand a couple of times. If this fails, a bystander closer to the intended person will be asked to wave to gain attention. Within a Deaf environment, a person may bang on a table with their fist so that the vibrations will attract attention. If we want the attention of Deaf children, we can flick lights on and off, but there are certain norms involved in this process. If the flicking is really fast, they know the matter is urgent and they must respond right away. If we do the same thing more slowly, they will eventually look up, but perhaps only when they have finished a certain task.

When two Deaf people are together, each person is responsible for informing the other of any dangers. If both are communicating while walking on a sidewalk, each tells the other about oncoming traffic and light standards, mailboxes, and so on, that are in the way. This allows them to carry on communicating by looking at each other while also acquiring visual knowledge of the environment without having to constantly look at the surroundings.

Like their hearing counterparts, Deaf children and adults should be able to identify the prominent events and individuals in art, history and sports which make up an important part of Deaf heritage. This provides Deaf children with a sense of identity and cultural values. After all, most of us are motivated to learn about different people, their background, culture and even language, if we have a strong social foundation to begin with. The situation is no different for Deaf children.

An excellent book to have is *Deaf Heritage in Canada* by Clifton F. Carbin. An exploration of a distinctive, diverse and enduring culture, it tells the story of Deaf Canadians – the events, individuals and societal attitudes that have shaped their lives, and the impact they have had on our country. One of the people profiled is a friend of mine, Gary Malkowski, the first elected Deaf MPP in the history of the Ontario legislature and the first elected born-Deaf politician to use ASL in conducting parliamentary business. Gary has set an extraordinary example for Deaf people from all walks of life. One reporter called him "the real thing," someone straight from the community. He does not think of being Deaf as an illness or a deficiency, or something he wants to "cure."

When studying the Arts, all students can learn about Deaf artists. One example is Douglas Tilden who is known as San Francisco's Father of Sculpture. There is a book about him called *The Man and His Legacy* by Mildred Albronda. His monuments, constructed as San Francisco grew to prominence in the late 19th century, are considered to be the greatest single legacy of public art in the San Francisco Bay area. He left a visual heritage in bronze as a testimony to that turbulent and magnificent era.

Schools must direct their focus to Deaf history, heritage and culture. Many times Deaf students' work is limited to the prescribed lesson plan and they do not get enough exposure to what is happening outside their world. Why? In large part, it is not because the students do not understand; it has more to do with the students' literacy levels and whether their teachers are fluent in sign language, familiar with Deaf issues and able to encourage their students to get involved in Deaf culture. Students need to increase their cultural and critical literacy levels.

Hearing parents can look at how Deaf parents interact with Deaf children to help them raise their own Deaf child. They can talk to other Deaf people and try to learn ASL. If this is not possible, they can take the time to do written communication with their Deaf child, as my Dad did with me. At a time when there were virtually no closed-captioned TV programs, Dad would sit down beside me and write down everything that was being said on TV. If there were disagreements or debates, we would write back and forth for hours at a time. This interaction helped me develop important debating and writing skills.

Many important decisions are made for Deaf children based on the language norms of hearing individuals. Sometimes Deaf children are discriminated against because their intellectual capacities and growth are determined by these norms. How can we best nurture Deaf children and at the same time support their development socially, emotionally and physically in ways that parallel the same development in hearing children? Dawn, a hearing parent, asked me this when she began to doubt if she was doing the right thing by sending her Deaf son, Matt, to a Deaf school. She knew he seemed well adjusted and very happy there but when he asked if he could get a hearing aid, Dawn wondered if she had made a mistake. She was concerned that any Deaf child who has some hearing ability or wants to have a hearing aid should go to a hearing school.

My answer to her was this: I have two hearing children. I know that they are hearing, so I support their environment and their needs. I make sure they go to a hearing school, I make sure there is music in the house, I make sure they have ample opportunities to interact with hearing children and have lots of contact with our hearing family members. By doing so, I support their environment. I encourage them to move within both the hearing community and the Deaf community. I feel Dawn is doing the right thing by supporting Matt's environment. He is Deaf and needs the Deaf environment. When he wants to, he can enter and experience the hearing community – which he is already doing – to have his needs met. By the phrase, "needs being met," I mean that he is content as a Deaf child, allowed to use his own language, and allowed to make Deaf friends – all of which encourages him to be curious about the hearing world.

It is important to realize that hearing aids are not like glasses. They do not correct hearing: they only amplify sound. For some people, the amplification is enough to hear sounds that allow for understanding, but most Deaf people still cannot hear whole words or sentences. They must work extra hard to fill in the missing gaps and absent sounds. This does not mean that a hearing aid should not be used as it may help provide a link to elements of hearing culture, such as going to a musical concert, that the Deaf person may be able to explore.

If Matt was taken out of a Deaf school and only wore

hearing aids he would have very little exposure to Deaf culture. He would miss out on the experiences that Deaf culture has to offer him such as involvement in team sports and education. He would also miss out on the values inherent in the Deaf community.

When a new immigrant comes to Canada, we do not assume that the person will assimilate totally into the new culture and leave the old culture behind in the country of origin. It is natural for a person to maintain cultural links such as traditions, religion and language. This multicultural environment is actually strongly accepted and encouraged in Canada. Heritage languages are taught in some high schools. Partaking in a second culture allows for a deeper understanding of differing points of view and a greater appreciation for people of different ethnic and cultural backgrounds.

Music can be explored by Deaf individuals and Deaf children should have exposure to all kinds of music. Give them drums; let them explore rhythm, which is not affected by hearing. There is nothing wrong with a different way of playing music. Many Deaf people also enjoy dancing and singing in ASL. Hearing people may ask, does Deaf culture encourage music? True, music is not part of Deaf culture, but it is with us everywhere and every day. We do not value music the same way hearing people do. I'm not Chinese, but I enjoy Chinese food from time to time. People borrow language, customs and values from other cultures. Let children experience everything the world has to offer them.

I would like to share an incident that occurred to me which parallels Dawn's dilemma. When my hearing son was two years old, a social worker from the hospital dropped by our house without an appointment. I asked her how she knew about us. She said she was referred by the hospital. Although she proudly announced that she knew sign language, she was not able to finger-spell with any ease. My son, in contrast, could sign whole sentences. He and I could communicate very well. He could also talk with hearing people. But in this case, it seemed that my son knew instinctively that he was "different." When asked through written communication why she had come, the social worker explained that she was doing a survey and wanted to find out how my son's language was progressing. In other words, she wanted to know how he was doing being brought up in a Deaf environment. In response to her questions, my son instinctively would not speak. Then, because she could see only what she could hear, which in this case was nothing at all, she advised me that our babysitter should teach him speech.

I felt insulted, told her that she did not know her job and showed her out of the house. However well intentioned, the attitude demonstrated by this social worker made me feel inadequate, even though I know I was and am a good parent. It is as if society was second-guessing all the hard work and sacrifices I had made for my children, just because I am Deaf. This episode illustrates why it can be dangerous for hearing parents to make decisions based on linguistic assumptions rather than linguistic knowledge.

Let's consider another all too familiar scenario, this one from organized sports. When a Deaf child is a member of a hearing team, he or she frequently ends up warming the bench, not because of the child's ability but because the coach does not have the time or the language training necessary to explain what is expected from that child. Why not let that child join an all-Deaf team? Many Deaf children have done just that. They love to compete against hearing teams, because doing so makes them feel part of the spirit and no one is left out. As was mentioned earlier, we have World Deaf Sports, organizers of the Deaf Olympics which are held every four years. Deaf schools provide a vehicle for community development and independence, allowing students to take a leadership role in the Deaf world. There are also Deaf organizations at the local, provincial, national and even international level. In addition, there are Deaf political organizations which advocate for educational rights and job opportunities, and opportunities for volunteering with the Deaf Olympics, the World Federation of the Deaf, World Sports and cultural events at all levels.

Language is an instinctive human system of communicating thoughts, feelings and desires. Language contains our collective identities because it shapes the way we think and embodies all our cultural assumptions. Without words, without a common language, we simply cannot establish useful human contact with those around us.

We do not develop language on our own; a group using the language transmits it to us. The language of Deaf people is natural sign language – that is communicating by signing. There are different sign languages all over the world, depending upon the country you live in. American Sign Language is the most conspicuous type used in Canada and the United States. The *Langue des Signes Québécois* is a French sign language used in Quebec, New Brunswick and surrounding areas. There is also a Chinese Sign Language, British Sign Language, Swedish Sign Language and many others. A tremendous amount of research on bilingual education indicates that the key to successful learning of a second language is to introduce the primary language early and to maintain it. Primary language learning is valuable not only in its own right but also for the crucial role it plays in learning a second language.

JOANNE S. CRIPPS

Culture, on the other hand, encompasses more than language; it incorporates traditions, identity, history, values and cultural norms or expectations for behaviour. If we look at Deaf people as a linguistic minority and assume that they have attended residential schools all their lives, we will see that they use their natural sign language; have a clear sense of identity (they are not afraid to be Deaf); have established a set of values (they understand the way Deaf children learn in school and the importance of Deaf children meeting other Deaf children, for example); and follow their own traditions such as annual sports tournaments in bowling, baseball, volleyball and darts where young and old play together and renew acquaintances and friendships. Nowhere can these things be learned by young Deaf people as easily as they can at Deaf residential schools.

Deaf culture, rich in history and tradition, makes life comfortable for Deaf individuals. We enjoy immense benefits from our own shared culture. It adds richness to communication and relationships and enables us to share feelings, thoughts, perceptions, beliefs and information in ways that are truly accessible. For these reasons, it is critical that Deaf children are accorded the right to interact fully with other Deaf children and adults.

How can parents ensure their Deaf child can take full advantage of language and culture?

- Expose children early to both cultures, Deaf and hearing. Many families speak two languages at home. As long as parents keep the two languages separate, their child will not become confused. He or she will have acquired one language and learned a second language. The child

44

can then become bilingual.

• Expose children to bilingual-bicultural Deaf education so they can learn about two languages and two cultures. This fosters an appreciation of who they are as individuals as well as acceptance and appreciation of others. It is about understanding one's own cultural values as well as those of others. It is about digging deep inside ourselves to understand and develop our full abilities and becoming empowered and confident enough to express them fully.

CHAPTER FIVE

SOCIAL GROUND

Am I Deaf?

Am I deaf?
Am I like you?
You call me deaf.

I do not understand
Why I am deaf.

What is deafness?
How did I become deaf?
I did not know
The answers.

I asked different people to answer my questions
Yet they could not,
Forcing me to look up in books.
"Deaf – means?"
I still could not find the answer.

I had to sit and look in retrospect.
To discover this silent secret.

During my growing years
People down there taught me
To speak, lipread, act, think, love,
Play, and even play music,
Regardless if I could hear or not,

But they still identified me as deaf?

Not till my teenage years
When I participated in hearing groups

In tennis, swimming, and Girl Guides,
Did I begin to feel
That something was wrong with me.

When I was in the group,
Whenever the group went out to certain places
They tended to leave me out
Leaving me lonely and rejected.

When the group made a joke
And I could not follow
I still tried to laugh with them.
I had to keep my eyes on everyone
To keep up with the conversation
But in the end I was always lost...

Really, down inside of me
I did not feel too comfortable,
But I said "Never mind."

I tried to become assertive
In order to fit into the group.
But the question kept nagging at me:
"Am I deaf?"
I tried to ignore it
But in the end I couldn't.

Am I deaf?
Am I like you?

Remaining as an oral student,
I struggled to grasp
Knowledge and ideas
From the moving mouth.

Only little did I receive,
The rest was being carried away.

Am I deaf?

Not till five years ago
When my family immigrated to Canada
And I attended the school for the deaf,

Did I discover teachers who could sign.
It amazed me!

I was even astonished to see
That I could follow
Their sign language
Regardless of my limited exposure to it.

I could see their radiant faces
With moving hands in the air,
Freely expressing themselves in their own language.

Am I deaf?
Am I like you?

Sitting in the park,
Trying to figure out
Who I was,
An old man saw me contemplating.
He touched me gently and asked
"Are you deaf?"
I nearly jumped out of my skin.

"Yes, I am," I replied,
"And you?"

Patricia Shores
Sounds of the Soul

Patty wrote this poem when she was going through the transition from being a teenager to a young adult, searching for her identity and role in the community. She says she has led a productive life thanks to the encouragement and opportunities offered to her. She now lives in Switzerland and reports that there is work to do in order to provide the same opportunities for Swiss Deaf people that Deaf Canadians currently enjoy.

SOCIAL GROUND

SOCIAL GROUND* is a concept first introduced by Kurt Lewin who developed the theory after completing his doctoral studies in the Gestalt psychology tradition at the University of Berlin. His work greatly influenced Group Dynamics and other areas of social psychology that study attitudes. Lewin maintains that an individual's behaviour is determined by his or her contemporary life space, which is constituted not by the objective environment itself, but by the way the individual perceives it.

A person's social ground is the understanding that he or she is an individual who is also part of a wider minority social grouping. This concept applies to all people of every culture, religion and racial group. For example, a child can belong to a number of minorities: Black, Jewish, Deaf, Asian, physically disabled, obese, low-income, and so forth. How does society perceive this child? How is each group – not the particular child – seen by others? Society's views greatly affect children; thus it is even more important to be aware of and inform children about these

* I want to thank Dr. Richard Dart who introduced me to the Social Ground concept and provided me with his valuable insight.

51

perceptions. Children need to be equipped with the knowledge of who they are in a historical and cultural context. Social ground literally "grounds" the child by providing the background which relates specifically to him or her. Parents of minority children need to say to their child, "You are Deaf (Black, Jewish, etc.) and you will encounter name calling, prejudice and discrimination. You will feel excluded because you are part of a minority social group, and this is how society views and treats that group. There is nothing wrong with you. You are a wonderful individual, and society is wrong to treat you in such a way."

When children are not allowed to know, understand and accept their social ground, they may feel isolated. They may believe they do not fit in. The struggle to understand what it means to be Deaf has raised critical issues for many parents of Deaf children, particularly around the teaching of language skills and access to the Deaf community. In this regard a crucial decision has to be made: Should my child learn sign language or should my child learn to speak orally, as the hearing world does? We need to remind ourselves that oral language will isolate children from the Deaf community and in doing so limits their ability to identify with and participate in Deaf culture. Public notions of what it means to be Deaf are out of touch with the reality of the Deaf experience.

I work with Deaf children staying in residence at a Deaf school. One of my students, Cathy (not her real name), had been mainstreamed* in a hearing school and was recently transferred to the Deaf school. I asked her how she liked the Deaf school so far. She said, "Not bad." I asked if she liked to mingle with new Deaf friends. Her

---

* Mainstreaming refers to Deaf students who attend public school and take classes with hearing students. They may or may not have access to interpreting services, although in most cases these services are not provided.

nonchalant reply was, "In the future, I will be hearing. My mother told me." She seemed so sure she would become hearing.

In order to lay the foundations of a strong social ground, Cathy's parents would have been advised to:

(a) help her acknowledge she is Deaf and will remain Deaf;

(b) help her understand that because she is Deaf she will be treated differently than those who are hearing. She may be teased, talked about behind her back, left out, oppressed and not understood. When these things happen, Cathy needs to understand that historically, thousands of other Deaf people have been treated in the same way. "This is your social ground, Cathy," is one way of expressing this idea; and

(c) help her understand that her own value and worth is not defined by others' treatment of her.

I had another student, Bob (not his real name), who believed that he would become hearing and thus did not see any reason why he should learn to read and write. When I interviewed him at the hearing school, I told him that I am an adult and am still Deaf, that I have been Deaf since birth and will never be hearing. He did not believe me at first. It took some convincing.

If a child is born Deaf, his or her social ground can include Deaf culture, heritage and literature. Recent research studies have indicated that ASL in particular has its own literacy which is strong and alive. Lon Kuntz, Sam Suppalla, Jan Gemmill and Clayton Valli have all investigated various aspects of ASL poetry, ASL storytelling, ASL histories and English literacy.

Let's look at the definition of literacy. Literacy, according to *Webster's Unabridged Dictionary* means "to be literate" or "to be educated by having or showing extensive knowledge, experience or culture." Literacy is less about reading and writing per se (as pertains to English) than it is about ways of being in the world and ways of reasoning and making meaning around text.

In the not-so-distant past, ASL literacy was not thought about. When my two hearing children were growing up, my sister advised me to read stories to them every night. I was shocked. Do I have to read them three or four books every night? She said, "Yes," reminding me that our parents read her stories every night. But I couldn't do it. I did not know how to read to hearing children just as my parents did not know how to read stories to me.

Deaf children need Deaf all-visual environments – ASL, lots of printed materials, closed-captioned programs on television and the stimulation provided by other Deaf children. I have often advised counsellors who are both hearing and Deaf to read stories to the residential students at bedtime. Many of them, however, do not have the necessary skills or training to effectively read stories in ASL. Deaf counsellors did not have the opportunity when they were growing up to have stories read to them. Their experiences were limited, and thus their training was also limited. Yet storytelling is an important part of children's literacy, and literacy is essential to the Deaf child's social ground.

A holistic approach for a bilingual-bicultural environment in home, school and residence focuses on four main areas: language, culture, identity and learning. This promotes a creative path for students to learn more about their history, culture, language and identity – who they are. It is important that Deaf children are exposed to various forms of literature to experience the freedom of expression and the opportunity of learning they provide. Literature does not exist in school alone; it must also be found at home and in residence, within the hearing community as well as the Deaf community. How do parents achieve this?

David Bobier is a hearing parent of two Deaf children. In *Signing On: Adopting a Cultural Perspective*, Bobier put it well: "ASL is a language that we value for many reasons. Because it is a visual language, we can be ourselves and express ourselves completely. We do not have to constantly clarify or simplify what we are saying. We are able to share abstract information when creating stories, poems, or other genres of the language. We also are able to provide content that reflects the kinds of cultural and life experiences and background that we hold in common. We use our language to share our literature which is related to our experiences and background with Deaf children and adults. We give our children a better understanding of our history. We also use it to increase their understanding of what it is like to be a victim of audism and oppression. ASL can be described in terms of both its literature and its linguistic features."

I want to expand a bit more on ASL literature. It is the telling of poetry, stories, drama, tales and legends that are passed down from one generation to the next by culturally Deaf people. ASL literature plays a primary role in the Deaf community as it is the vehicle in which our values, history, culture and language are passed on. It provides us with a rich understanding and knowledge of what is happening within our environment and the people who live in it. It helps us to examine and understand our personal experiences, and to take comfort in knowing that other Deaf people experience the same things we experience. It also introduces us to new experiences. It allows Deaf children to develop values and morals, an important role of heritage languages according to the Common Curriculum

JOANNE S. CRIPPS

(1995) governing the school system in the province of Ontario. ASL literature stimulates Deaf children's imagination and curiosity. It provides the opportunity for "playing" with language. We use ASL literature to build our history and pride in our language, identity and culture. We often share ABC stories, number stories, Deaf legends and other literature within the Deaf community. We use jokes, stories and riddles, both as a way to identify and as a way to escape from different forms of oppression.

It is not surprising that ASL literature has attracted the attention of scholars. One has looked at its origins and the impulses behind it, observing that it arises from the thoughts, emotions and experiences of culturally Deaf people (Byrne, 1996). Another has examined its place within the "oral literature" tradition (Bahan, 1991). ASL literature has also been studied in terms of the genres it includes and the special content that concerns its creators: Deaf characters, Deaf culture, Deaf identity and Deaf experiences (Jacobowitz, 1998). It is part of the larger Deaf heritage which, similar to other heritages, includes works of art, cultural achievements and folklore of culturally Deaf people that have been passed on from earlier generations of culturally Deaf people (CCSD, 1999). And a heritage, as we have seen, gives a person his or her social ground.

Heather Gibson, Deaf Vice-Principal at the E.C. Drury School for the Deaf in Milton, Ontario, developed the following list for the goals of ASL literature.*

Language Goals to:
• facilitate students' bilingual language learning in natural settings;
• provide hands-on learning experience in ASL

---

* Adapted from the Learning Centre for Deaf Children, Framingham, MA, "Language Arts Curriculum Resource Guide for Teachers in a Bilingual Bicultural School with Deaf Students," 1993.

literature;
- enhance students' appreciation of the artistic uses of ASL; and
- provide students with exciting opportunities to develop their early literacy skills.

Culture Goals to:
- expose students to their Deaf heritage; and
- provide Deaf students opportunities to interact and to work cooperatively on projects that address their culture and language.

Identity Goals to:
- expose students to Deaf role models;
- introduce students to artists as mentors;
- provide students with opportunities for creative self-expression and self-exploration;
- help students develop pride and self-esteem; and
- provide artistically-gifted students with an opportunity to develop their gifts.

Learning Goals to:
- teach students that learning can be fun, creative and active; and
- teach students to explore their own interests through a variety of artistic forms of literature.

Where do we go from here? Where are the resources? Here are some recommendations to help your Deaf child find his or her social ground:

- First of all, take up ASL classes. There no question about it. From the day you find out your child is Deaf, start ASL classes right away despite the advice you may get on how to raise

your child. DO NOT WAIT UNTIL ANOTHER
METHOD FAILS. Natural sign language is not
a "method." Make the most of it. If you are
determined to teach your child speech, do it
during enrichment classes. If you want to use
the oral approach, that is fine, but you don't
know whether this is the path your child will
take. The oral approach is a method. ASL is not
a method. It is a language. Nothing is more
rewarding than being able to communicate with
your child and having your child communicate
with you.

• Find a Deaf mentor who uses ASL and can
lead you to the Deaf community. This mentor's
responsibility will be to foster language interaction. There is a famous expression which I can't
say any better: Experience is the best teacher. I
know a hearing family who invites a Deaf mentor's family to family camps. The family and
their mentor family take turns sleeping over on
weekends. If there are problems with homework
or school, the Deaf family mentors and the hearing family help one another.

• Attend workshops and seminars to improve
communication and increase your children's
exposure to ASL literature, Deaf literature and
English literature. A hearing mother explained
to me how her family reads at bedtime. The
father reads the story aloud and the mother
interprets in ASL, bringing all the siblings, both
hearing and Deaf, together to read the story at
the same time.

• Get together with other bilingual-bicultural parents to set up a support network to help each other and pursue goals together.

• Use ASL videotapes in the home. Your local library can order Deaf Heritage literature with videotapes and books so that you, your family and your child can enjoy the same literature.

• Use visual technology, such as TTYs, lights flashing to indicate the ringing phone or door bell, a closed-captioned decoder on the TV as soon as you find out your child is Deaf. Get a video camera to record stories. Make a video-tape to record your family history, explaining each person's date and place of birth, and background, featuring an interpreter or yourself, if your signing skills are good. Your Deaf child will love to watch it again from time to time to remember names, events and other details.

• Have your Deaf child's siblings take up ASL classes. If this is a problem, try finding a Deaf mentor to arrange for an older Deaf student to teach ASL to the hearing siblings.

• Get involved in Deaf community events that are geared to your Deaf child's age.

• Invite Deaf friends into your home. Invite Deaf guests to dinner or to a barbecue. Your child will love it and will feel important because "my hearing parents" invite Deaf persons into our home.

JOANNE S. CRIPPS

Hints for Telling Stories to Deaf Children

Reading stories to Deaf children through the use of ASL is just as beneficial as reading aloud to hearing children. Not only do they enjoy stories, Deaf children also learn many valuable lessons including morals and values, creative use of the imagination, enjoyment of story time, turn-taking and word recognition.

When reading a story to a Deaf child, the reader must translate the English sentences into ASL. Allow time for viewing the pictures and asking questions. Allow time for the child to read the printed words. Through use of body movement and facial expression, the storyteller can adeptly become many different characters from the book. Vary your signing positions in the same manner as you would alter the tone and inflection of your voice for a hearing child. Signing with the child allows him or her to become involved in the story-telling experience. Daily ASL storytelling is a critical part of encouraging early literacy in a Deaf child. You should also ask questions to make sure the children understand and answer questions that the children pose.

Reading books and ASL storytelling are creative, imaginative and interactive ways to learn.

CHAPTER SIX

THE HOME ENVIRONMENT

Deaf Children's Graceful Little Hands

I love Deaf children.
Each time I stop by the school
Little hands tap tap on my knee
With sparkling eyes looking up at me
And signing little fingers in the air.
Oh, I love their graceful little hands.

I love the joys of friendship true
That grow in peaceful silence
Among the Deaf children there.
Oh, I love their graceful little hands
Freely giving, loving, and sharing...

Christine Spink-Mitchell
Sounds of the Soul

Christine is an ASL Specialist at the Manitoba School for the Deaf. She is a highly motivated person who brings a sense of humour and warmth to her work. She creates an open, dynamic and enjoyable environment for everyone. A great ASL storyteller, she is fascinated with Deaf children's small signing hands.

THE HOME ENVIRONMENT

I T HAS OFTEN been said that the hardest and most important job in the world is being a parent. Parents take their responsibilities seriously; they want to raise their children to be healthy, happy citizens. This is also an aim of the United Nations Convention, which states, with respect to parental care, "Both parents have common responsibilities for the upbringing and development of the child. Parents or guardians have the primary responsibility, with the best interests of the child as their basic concern." We need now to investigate what the best interests of the Deaf child are.

Parental support of a Deaf child in the home environment can have lasting affects. Communication between parents and child is vital. New technology now provides wake up alarms, TTYs, closed-caption decoders and flashing-light doorbells, things that empower Deaf children to live more independently in their home environment.

A lot of parents ask me, "How do we teach Deaf children to love reading?" According to Jan Gemmill, a Deaf English professor at Gallaudet University (an internationally recognized higher learning institution for the Deaf located in Washington, D.C.), 85 percent of Deaf children have never read a book just for the pleasure of reading. To them, reading is something they are told to do in order to be assessed and evaluated.

Looking back, I must admit this is consistent with my own experience. I began going to school at the age of five. Each day my education consisted of speech training. We were taught to speak a few words – once we were able to speak those words "perfectly" we moved on to learning more words. To me, it was a chore, not an education that taught me the sheer joy of learning. I could understand a few printed words but wasn't able to connect those words to the written language.

I really started reading at the age of twelve. Home for the summer holidays, I was bored because I had very little communication with my family. I started going to the library, which was just around the corner, almost every day. I began with a book that was designed for grade one readers and gradually read more difficult books. My older sister, Marlene, was a big help even though she could only finger-spell to me. She had a lot of patience and she was an A+ student in English. When I asked her what a word meant, she did not just give me its meaning. She showed me how to use that word in three or four, sometimes five, different sentences. I was impatient. I just wanted to get on with what that one word meant. But no, she'd sit me down and explain the word to me fully, slowly increasing my reading ability word by word. I was proud when I was able to read the Nancy Drew books – like most girls my age, once I started, I couldn't stop reading them.

Reading becomes more purposeful when students are encouraged to discuss the material they've read and compare it with their own experiences. Reading incorporates many skills: thinking, inferring, analyzing, predicting and comparing information. It is also important to realize that reading and writing are interrelated. Reading requires purpose, motivation and incentive. Readers use the known to teach themselves the unknown. William Faulkner's advice is particularly important to a Deaf reader: "Read, read, read. Read everything – trash, classics, good and bad – and see how they do it, like a carpenter who works as an apprentice and studies the master. Read! You'll absorb it. Then write."

Parents can make reading fun using table games, puppetry, ASL videotapes and rap combining drums and ASL poetry. (See Appendix for list of resources.) If you are a hearing parent, use a TTY to talk to Deaf adults. Let the Deaf adult know that your child is sitting beside you while you are typing back and forth. It will help reinforce the English content of your child's education. An important note: the more fluent Deaf children are in ASL – their primary language – the easier it is for them to learn English as a second language. They will need a great deal of exposure to written English, to learn how it is written and how we can play around with the words.

I do not favour the Fitzgerald method,* a reading technique in which Deaf readers are expected to learn to read by memorizing English sentence structures. The main problem with this method is that it was used for spoken English by most teachers, so the natural generative aspect of the language is missing. Reading and language use should be fun. Teachers who apply the Fitzgerald method rigidly lose sight of how language can be generated creatively to express important ideas.

We must look closely at each individual child. Consider a Deaf five-year-old boy who just started school

* See *Hearing and Deafness*, 4th edition, 1978, Holt, Rinehart and Winston, pp. 470-473.

with no language with which to express himself. The boy was not exposed to ASL at home, where communication consisted of gestures, lip-reading (to a limited degree) and pointing. He was becoming increasingly more aggressive because of his frustration with not being able to communicate meaningfully. During homework time, he was expected to read children's books and write a daily journal. Now, step back and assess this situation. Ask yourself, why is this child becoming more aggressive?

If we are to really understand what each child needs, we need to stand in his or her shoes. Before any child can read, that child must first have a language base. Hearing children first acquire the spoken language before learning to read. The same experience must apply to Deaf children. They need an environment which encourages natural language acquisition, specifically ASL, in order to provide them with a language-based foundation.

Let us return to that aggressive little boy. I instructed the adults in his world to communicate with him in ASL only. He needs a language. Forget the reading, forget the writing. The school started using ASL with him and, during homework time, provided him with ASL storytelling videotapes. We took the approach that it is impossible to discipline a child if he or she does not have a language or cannot understand consequences. Within three weeks, once he started communicating and understanding the world around him, the boy's aggressive behaviour lessened. At this point, reading and writing were re-introduced to him with much greater success.

Learning and using ASL does not mean that English is unimportant. On the contrary, in recent years a great deal of research has focused on ASL literacy and how it can enhance learning English. Literacy in ASL provides Deaf people with knowledge, culture, life experience and the ability to express a language. ASL is rich with stories, poetry, legends and folktales, in much the same way that English is. The goal of ASL literacy is to encourage the ability to sign fluently, providing the Deaf child with a wide vocabulary and the confidence to express himself or herself clearly, as well as to understand signing by others. I firmly believe that parents have the right to raise their children in accordance with their own values and lifestyle but, if their child is Deaf, sign language, interacting with other Deaf children and exposure to Deaf role models are their basic human needs. Deaf and hearing parents, the Deaf community, hearing allies and professionals can work together to interweave a bridge of support for Deaf children to help them realize their full potential.

How can we best meet the interests of the Deaf child within the home environment? Is the Deaf child interacting with other Deaf children and Deaf role models? If not, then an alternative nurturing system can be put into place. Articles 14 and 30 of the United Nations Convention on the Rights of the Child concerning freedom of thought, conscience and religion state, "Children of minority communities and/or of indigenous origin have the right to enjoy their own culture, practice their own religion and use their own language." Living at or even near a residential school would allow the Deaf child to interact with other Deaf peers. The child's language and cultural needs could also be met in this setting.

Although it may be difficult to face, it may be best to send your child to attend a Deaf residential school. Some Deaf children travel many miles to attend school during the week and return home for weekends and holidays. This may seem frightening to a hearing parent who has never been through the experience before. There are many questions and concerns that will go through a parent's mind:

What about the safety of my child? What about the family morals and values that should be taught to my child? How will I keep close contact with the teachers to know if my child's homework has been completed? And especially, how can I send my Deaf child away, all alone, for such long periods of time?

Parents must choose carefully when deciding on a residential school. Each residence has a staff that should be willing to talk about any questions and concerns. Each individual family situation must be looked at carefully and will result in different answers based on each student's individual needs. I will describe the advantages of attending a residential school based on my own experiences.

I was always well taken care of. The residence counsellors treated all students as though we were one big family. We had rules we abided by that kept us safe and helped reflect our family values and morals. There were always consequences to our poor behaviour and our parents were always made aware of what was happening with us. To me, residential school is really like a private boarding school. It is not a treatment centre whose residents are isolated from the outside.

It was a great joy to freely communicate and interact with the other students in the residence. I never felt isolated, always knew what was going on around me and I participated in sports and activities. Although when I went to residential school there were no Deaf role models, there are many available to today's Deaf students. This is a great opportunity for students to see what their futures could hold.

I believe in residential schools; however, I am well aware that all family situations are different. Some Deaf children may not be able or may not want to leave home. Their best interests must be met in other ways.

Some families have actually moved closer to residential schools so that their children could be bused there daily. This decision must take into account many factors: Where is the school? Are there jobs or career opportunities for the parents? What is the new community like? Is the family able to afford such a move?

Even if neither option is available, parents can still offer many things at home to make the environment more conducive to their child's involvement in Deaf culture.

When I was a child, my family was advised not to learn sign language because doing so would interfere with my ability to learn to talk. To understand what was said, I was expected to lip-read even, for example, when walking home from school I could not always see my friend's lips. At the dinner table, when everyone laughed, someone would need to explain the joke to me, but by that time it often was no longer very funny. In short, I was seen but seldom heard.

As children with a Deaf sibling grow up and go their separate ways, they may find it difficult if not impossible to maintain or establish a close relationship with their Deaf sister or brother. The parents of the Deaf child may feel inadequate or guilty for not learning ASL, regretting what they might have shared with their Deaf child. Let me share a recollection in which one of my hearing sisters, Mossie, gives her perspective:

> My sister is Deaf. Growing up, I really didn't know much about her. She went to a residential school for Deaf children where she made many friends. She lived there most of the time, so it was easy to understand why these friends are now like family to her.
>
> People used to ask me if I knew sign language,

and when I said "no," I felt really stupid. I had wanted to learn how to sign, but school representatives told my parents that, if we learned to sign, my sister would not learn how to speak. My friends and I thought it would be great to know how to sign because other people would not know what we were saying. We made up our own code of signs, but the funny thing was that we could not understand each other anyway.

Whenever my sister would come home from a lengthy stay at school, she would try to teach us sign language and would check to see if we had practiced finger-spelling. It must have been frustrating for her, but it was like a game to us. She stopped at some point maybe because she thought that we did not take her seriously. It didn't seem to matter whether she signed or used her voice to say something. If she thought I was not listening, she would ask, "What did I say?" I would have to repeat it – if I could.

Conversations one to one were slow, but at the family dinner table with eight people, it was impossible to include her in everything that was said. We never intentionally excluded her but, when more than one person was talking at once, it was very difficult to explain to her what was going on. When everyone was laughing, a condensed version of what was said somehow didn't sound funny anymore. By that time, the conversation had usually switched to another topic

It often seemed that my sister got to do anything she wanted to. Not that she was spoiled, but the rules always changed when she was home. We had to behave ourselves, be patient, try to understand why we couldn't get her back for things she did to us. I remember one time when I was sitting with my elbows on the dinner table. My sister suddenly picked up the knife and gave my elbows a good whack. I was furious, but she wasn't punished. She explained how unfair it was to her that we could do whatever we wanted at home and how strict her life was at school. It wasn't until much later that I learned that, at her school, her elbows were banged with a knife for the same reason.

Now, we find ourselves considering what it must have been like for her as a child – like the time when our father died and there were no inter-preters for the service. I find myself questioning why I was so unaware of issues that would have meant a great deal to Joanne.

It's only been in the last few years that I have started to learn ASL and understand Deaf cul-ture. Perhaps if we'd had the chance to play games together, tell stories and share experi-ences when we were young, we could have achieved much more. I find it's me who needs patience and understanding when I am with a group of Deaf people signing a mile a minute.

To grow up with a Deaf sister is really something very special to our family, even if we don't tell her this often enough.

How can parents help set up a nurturing and stimulating home for their Deaf child?

• Allow your child to be independent whenever possible. Your child should place his or her own order in a restaurant or fast food establishment, pay for purchases in a store, go to the library, make appointments to see doctors, etc.

• Get a TTY – it will help you and your child keep up daily phone conversations to stay abreast of issues.

• Post notes explaining where you are going and when you will be back. This allows your child to know what is happening, saves them time looking for you and also reinforces writing skills.

• Put a mirror on the wall of your child's room so that he or she can see who is entering the room. Instead of musical mobiles, install a lamp that reflects images around the room. Put up alphabet handshape charts and pictures of events happening at home.

• Use the closed captioning option on your TV and install a strobe light to indicate a fire alarm.

• Write down emergency numbers and show your child how to access the numbers and what to do in an emergency.

• Invite Deaf friends over to play board games.

CHAPTER SEVEN

ACCESS TO INFORMATION

In 1965, the United Nations Educational, Scientific and Cultural Organization (UNESCO) adopted the view that, rather than be an end in itself, literacy should be regarded as a way of preparing [humankind] for a social, civic and economic role that goes far beyond the limits of rudimentary literacy training consisting merely in the teaching of reading and writing.

"Literacy, Gateway to Fulfillment"
UNESCO Courier

ACCESS TO INFORMATION

A S ADULTS, WE are aware of the importance of free-dom of information. Even the United Nations Convention on the Rights of the Child states, "The child has the right to: express an opinion freely and have that opinion heard; [and] seek, receive and impart information and ideas of all kinds, through any media." Imparting information, opinions and ideas helps develop children's independence, self-esteem and knowledge, allowing them to grow into independent, responsible citizens.

In the wider society, access to information means: access to entertainment and other media for recreational and informative purposes; access to medical and security measures when an emergency arises (i.e. police, fire, ambulance); and access to all medical data, doctors and other medical staff on conditions affecting them. In fact, it means that individuals are able to know about everything that affects them personally, in whole or in part, and to broaden themselves through education and leisure. But what does access to information mean for Deaf children? Quite simply, it means that they and their parents should have the same opportunity to gain information as the hearing world does; more importantly, it means that they should have particular knowledge of relevance to the Deaf community. Deaf children often have to surmount obstacles to gain access to clear, concise information. Children who use ASL as their first language may have difficulties interacting with the hearing majority who speak and write English. They also do not get the opportunity to "overhear" (language, as well as information, is picked up incidentally, by listening to the radio or to people around you), which is what hearing children do throughout the day. Even when people communicate in ASL, the quality of the conversation will depend on the extent of their knowledge of sign language and any other information that can be conveyed through visible media.

Hearing children are able to access most information quite readily through interaction, overhearing and direct communication; however, Deaf children can be deprived of some information. Consider what often happens with school report cards. The Deaf child does not always understand report cards, as they are typically designed for parents. Deaf children may have difficulty reading the written English that is used. For this reason, we must encourage parents and children to discuss what the language used in the report cards means. There are ways to do this: perhaps by discussing the content with the teacher, using a videotape in sign language to explain the report, or getting an interpreter if full communication is not possible among all parties. All children must understand the meaning of their report cards, so that they can take ownership of their strengths and acknowledge their weaknesses.

Parents can help their Deaf children develop independence by allowing them to make their own decisions and then "voice" their opinions. For example, when Deaf children go into a restaurant with their hearing parents, it may be natural for the parents to order for their Deaf children. This takes away from their child's independence and prevents a perfect learning opportunity. Deaf children can learn how to interact (by pointing to pictures or by writing down their orders) with waiters and waitresses within a safe environment (with hearing parents who are there if needed).

Communication is essential for full access to information, yet most hearing individuals seem to take for granted the supposedly simple ability to communicate. For them, communication is primarily auditory; for Deaf individuals, it is largely visual. Not surprisingly, many conflicts arise from the differences in these perspectives. If teachers, for example, are not well trained in English literacy, they may not realize that Deaf children will use words that unconsciously reflect their cultural reality. A Deaf child might write something like "I feel I should complete this work" or "I feel the dog is sad." The teacher may change "feel" to "think," because the latter word sounds more confident. However, the child may be deliberately using language more in keeping with the visual or tactile senses, e.g. "feel" as opposed to "think." This is why all of us, teachers in particular, need to be very sensitive in correcting the words which Deaf children choose to tell their stories.

Very few resources are presently available that encourage or even express and relate Deaf culture. Although ASL cannot be used in written form, the culture of the people who use ASL can be presented through various forms of literature. Instead of using reading material at home or in school that states, "The children ran to the door when they heard the doorbell," look for books that affirm Deaf culture by writing, "The children saw the flashing light and then ran to the door." By choosing and reading the most appropriate materials, Deaf children will feel a greater sense of self worth, and at the same time they will learn about Deaf culture.

In order to gain access to information about their immediate world and the larger world, Deaf people need a richer visual environment. Hearing people gain a great deal of information from the spoken word. This is a significant issue from the Deaf perspective. Deaf children would greatly benefit from a more visual environment, including open-captioned TV screens, and TTYs in airports, malls and government buildings. These are places rich in information that is crucial to the people who attend or visit them.

The idea of equal access to information also comes into play when Deaf children mainstreamed in a hearing school are not informed of Deaf residential schools where they could be in contact with a larger Deaf population. We are obliged to let them know as much as possible about these schools so that they can come to know and interact with Deaf peers and role models, eventually deciding for themselves the direction of their education and their life. We seem to believe that all children have a right to express an opinion on matters affecting them and to have that opinion heard. But do we practice what we preach in regard to Deaf children? Too often it is impossible for Deaf children to express their opinion in a group of hearing friends and classmates. Deaf children have the right to the strong self confidence that comes from expressing and establishing ownership of opinions. One way to help Deaf children participate in such discussions is to use an interpreter, especially if the rest of the group is hearing. However, we must remember that interpreters do not replace spontaneous social development. Deaf children have the right to enjoy the same benefits of verbal interaction as hearing children do; in fact, they learn a great deal of their language from such interactions.

Consider, as another example, a student group which calls a meeting with a school's administration team. Now, let's say that the administration is all hearing and that there are only two or three Deaf students. Unconsciously, the hearing individuals conduct the meeting according to their norms, with several people occasionally talking all at once. The Deaf students are at a decided disadvantage. They may be left out of the debate entirely because they are unable to follow the flow of the meeting. This type of proceeding needs to be modified to ensure that Deaf students feel they are important participants in the discussion. One ground rule would be to require the group's members to raise a hand in order to indicate their desire to say something. Using an interpreter is possible, but it demands a bit more time and patience in order to avoid a situation where hearing individuals offer their opinions in quick succession while the Deaf students working with an interpreter are trying to catch up with the rapid flow of ideas. Cultural conflicts will no doubt arise in the process, but if we make an effort, such meetings can be productive for all parties.

Two other examples deserve their own discussions, I believe. One pertains to medical information and the other – perhaps surprisingly – is the teaching and practice of religion.

The Medical Environment

It is important to make Deaf children aware that they can contact medical establishments, police and fire stations through TTY. In emergency situations Deaf children should know how to use the TTY and how to access the proper help.

79

JOANNE S. CRIPPS

Access to health care services is a right for all children; however, few may consider that knowledge about one's own health is also a right. Article 24.2(e) of the United Nations Convention on the Rights of the Child ensures that all segments of society, in particular parents and children, are informed, have access to education and are supported in the use of basic knowledge of child health and nutrition.

Consider a medical scenario: Selena is a Deaf child suffering from a variety of health problems. She goes to see the doctor often and sometimes has to stay in the hospital for extended periods. On one occasion, she is taken to the hospital in an ambulance. She lies on a bed while, all around her, people are talking and staring at her. They seem to be discussing her situation but no one stops to explain what is going on. She is fearful and anxious.

Selena wonders, "What are they talking about? Am I very sick? They all look so serious. Here comes my mom. She's not stopping to talk with me either; she's saying something to the doctors and the nurses. Now she is looking at me with a funny smile. What's wrong with me?"

Selena's case is not unique. My mother recounted an incident which occurred when I was a youngster. She wrote, "I took her to a specialist to identify whether or not she was Deaf. The doctor there came into the room and said, 'Strip off all her clothing except for the panties.' As I started to remove her clothing, Joanne started to cry as if she'd been stripped of her dignity."

Fear and a loss of dignity are not the only problems Deaf children face in their medical care. A lack of knowledge of Deaf issues and a lack of competent Deaf or hearing interpreters can sometimes lead to misdiagnosis, particularly in cases of abuse or neglect. For this reason alone, Deaf children who receive medical treatment have the right to skilled interpreters or to direct contact with a person who can sign. They have a right to participate in the discussion of their plan of care. They should not be left out because they do not seem to know how to communicate, because everyone thinks they will not understand, or because it is more convenient for everyone not to include them in the process. The rights of children in the medical environment have attracted considerable attention and discussion in the last few years; Deaf children must not be excluded from this process.

How can some of these problems be solved? Well, medical professionals can help by ensuring that they have access to qualified Deaf professionals for advice. They can check with their local hospitals and other health care facilities to see if they have a TTY and a list of interpreters to contact. Are the administrators of these places aware of the phone relay service and how to access it? At the very least, nurses and doctors must take the extra time to explain the diagnosis and procedures to their Deaf patients before they begin treatment. Parents must also be vigilant. Expect your doctor to take the time to explain treatments to your Deaf child. Locate all of the facilities which will help. If facilities are not available, indicate to the proper authorities that these services are not only beneficial but also essential.

Even when doctors recognize the need to communicate with their young Deaf patients, however, difficulties can still arise. Another example stands out. In this case, a mother asked the ear, nose and throat specialist to bring in an ASL-interpreter to explain the surgical process required for her five-year-old son. But the specialist did not see the need for one, saying that in a hearing world, her son would have to learn how to live in a hearing way. For their part, the nurses all felt that the mother was being overprotective. It would seem that the doctor and the nurses in this situation considered that this request represented a privilege instead of a right.

As a parent who wants the best for your child, it is only natural to press for things you feel are important. Make sure the doctor knows that an interpreter must be present. Be your child's advocate. You need to make people aware of issues they have never had to encounter before.

Hearing children often have the opportunity to get information (even if it is overheard) in the hospital. Professionals involved need to take the time to explain procedures to Deaf children. Unfortunately, Deaf children receiving medical treatment often do not even know their doctor or nurse by name.

Whether the necessary medical information is written or explained through an interpreter or a competent signer, we must remember one thing: it is always worthwhile to take the time to explain. Some Deaf patients prefer to communicate by using paper and pen. Others prefer a professional interpreter, while still others can talk and want to do so. Finally, we must always remember that patients should be the ones to choose the way in which they wish to communicate.

Children in hospital, especially Deaf children, can be fearful of the medical environment. That is all the more reason why they need to know who is looking after them and how long their visit will be. They should have access to family and friends, particularly if they are going to stay for a long time. How can we create a friendlier atmosphere for Deaf children, so that it doesn't matter that the hospital is a hearing environment? One possibility would be to have medical schools offer seminars by Deaf presenters on issues relevant to Deaf culture and community. A more immediate solution would be to provide hospitals with

TTYs and decoders. It is also advisable to enlist the services of a Deaf advocate so that parents will know how to stand up for their Deaf children's rights when dealing with medical professionals.

Deaf children's right to complete information becomes critical when we examine the various options for medical intervention: cochlear implants; auditory verbal therapy; trips to audiologists for hearing aids; therapy sessions with speech language pathologists, etc. Cochlear implants consist of parts worn outside the body (a microphone headset, external transmitter coil and a speech processor) and parts that are surgically implanted (an internal receiver and an electrode-array wire) behind the ear. The details of this operation are somewhat complicated, but the process of using a cochlear implant takes about as much time as a normal listener would require to perceive sound; however, this surgical procedure does not restore the child's hearing to normal. In fact, the signal received by the child is not similar to what he or she would receive from a hearing aid, if that were an option. It is an electronic signal the child must learn over time to interpret, a process which involves discriminating sounds from one another, recognizing their source and comprehending their meaning.

Although this issue overlaps almost all of the main considerations of this book, it is most relevant to the concepts of general access and freedom of information. Perhaps this is because cochlear implants cater to either our optimistic belief in technological answers or to our assumption that this procedure will offer Deaf children the kind of access they are supposed to want and require because it is assumed that Deaf people will naturally want to become part of the hearing world. However, these assumptions ignore some of the practical and ethical implications of medical intervention. Are parents fully informed of the risks, benefits and alternatives? Is it ethical to perform surgery on children, given that we still lack solid information about the advantages and disadvantages of cochlear implants? Are we not incorrectly assuming that Deaf children are "unhealthy" and need to be operated on? And, finally, how can we be sure that the child will approve of this operation when he or she grows up?

To be fair, the medical establishment has never touted cochlear implants as a cure for deafness, but the limitations and consequences of these implants have only recently been debated as fully and openly as they should. Apart from the problems associated with interpreting the signal generated by these devices, we should remember that only "normal" profoundly Deaf children with good attention spans would be likely candidates for implants. This creates biased statistics in favour of the implants' effectiveness. The selection process itself involves a number of tests and counselling sessions with both the proposed recipient and his or her family.

The ultimate decision about the cochlear implants remains with the parents, and this is where one significant problem begins. Cochlear implants are considered abusive by their opponents who argue that the procedure is promoted by doctors who do not see the spirit of the Deaf child. In addition, implants bring economic benefits to those in control (speech and language pathologists, oral teachers, social workers and psychologists), a form of economic exploitation. If you are the parent of a Deaf child considering an implant, have you ever wondered why the medical establishment does not make it a rule to ask you to meet Deaf adults first? Despite the best efforts of the cochlear implant team to provide relevant and impartial information and consultation, the members of this team may take an approach that reflects the biases of the hearing world. For example, the team members could quite unintentionally appeal to the understandable desire of parents to open a communication window for their child early in the child's language-learning process (a window that nevertheless might close partially or entirely with age). However, what we should remember here is that the same window can be opened just as early, if not earlier, by sign language and interaction with Deaf people.

Parents have the right the right to receive full information – both good and bad – regarding cochlear implant operations. This includes interviewing cochlear implant recipients. Often Deaf professionals, stuck in the middle, are not allowed to give opinions or information on this controversial issue. Some of them will not speak their minds because of the complications of the process. They may not want to hurt parents for making the decision to implant. They may not want to take responsibility for the decision. What if this child grows up to be a Deaf adult who is angry about the cochlear implant? They would ask why their parents and the Deaf consultants did not intervene.

I was in Austria in 1995 during the XII Congress of the World Federation of the Deaf (WFD). Their theme was Towards Human Rights. At the end of the week, WFD had a panel meeting to determine whether they should bend a little on their opposition to cochlear implants.

One man, very angry, stood up on the stage. He said he was from Brazil (I have forgotten his name and regret I did not write it down at the time). He had had two different cochlear implant operations, one on each side. He said both were worthless. No child should have to go through what he did. He explained what happened to him – a horrifying experience. He had the first implant when he was ten years old. He did not really know what was going on, except that he was told he would be able to hear. They operated on him. "Ten years old I am!! No power!! With bandages around my head." The operation was not successful but the medical team was able to convince his parents that a second operation would succeed because of newer technology. His family sold their house to finance the second operation. It was unsuccessful as well. The man wanted to have the cochlear implants removed but that meant paying even more money. He told the audience not to change their position about cochlear implants. "Think of the children: they are powerless," he said. It was a very moving message and I feel sad for him to this day.

This points out the problem of access to negative opinions or experiences related to cochlear implants. Parents may hear of success stories and promising progress reports, but do they get to hear the accounts of those who are less enthusiastic or downright miserable about the consequences of living with these implants? Some of these people have never felt fully included in either the hearing or the Deaf community. The point to be stressed here is not whether cochlear implants are good or bad, for this is something that parents must decide for themselves. What is more important is that parents have access to information from both perspectives because of the risks involved. A child is only a child once. The decision to operate will affect his or her entire life.

Religious Information

Access to religious information seems like a straight-forward matter; however, for Deaf children it may be more complicated. Deaf children need to be allowed full participation in the training and enjoyment of their faith. They have the right to full access to religious information, as do their hearing peers.

Here is a story both old and new. A family moves to Canada, bringing with them the social and religious values of the country they came from. In this family is a seventeen-year-old Deaf son, but the only communication between family members is based on immediate needs and duties, such as food and chores. Their strong family values focus on school and home, not on the need to have friends. They feel that being in a family and going to school are enough for their son. Unfortunately, this young man begins to have a lot of conflicts with his family. Both wanting and needing Deaf friends, he is glad of natural sign language and the many other aspects of Deaf culture that make such friendships possible. However, the family does not understand Deaf needs such as the need for a TTY and a decoder, while the son may feel but cannot explain his needs which differ dramatically from the old country's traditions and values. The family's perspective is that he has undergone too much "Canadian" influence; his perspective is that his family does not understand his thirst for communication and interaction. After a number of unpleasant clashes, he leaves home. Somewhat later, another family of the same faith, but all of them Deaf, agree to take in this young man. Only then does his mother begin to realize that the problem is not a racial or a religious issue, but a Deaf issue. Only then does she recognize that her son does indeed value both his own group and his religion; she also realizes that, by involving himself in a culture that satisfies his communication needs, he can lead a more fulfilling spiritual life.

Let me reassure all those who fear that Deaf culture will conflict with or undermine traditional religious teachings. Deaf culture is a way of life. It not only encourages independence in Deaf children but also gives them support

87

and enhances their social lives. People of different faiths belong to the Deaf community; their religious beliefs are a separate issue.

Religion is as important to Deaf people as it is to the hearing community. Deaf children need to have the same access to religious information as hearing children do. Unfortunately, it is a sad fact that most of them cannot participate in religious settings which are geared for a hearing congregation. The message from the minister, priest or rabbi is directed only to the hearing. Deaf children are expected to pay attention even if they have very little idea of what is being said, particularly at important family gatherings like weddings and funerals.

We need to ask ourselves some very important questions. Does a Deaf child in such a gathering need an interpreter? Is it really too expensive to get one? Doesn't this child need to know what is happening at this significant social event? If hearing children in the same environment are receiving all the essential information, why doesn't the Deaf child deserve the same kind of access?

If you have a Deaf child in this situation, you don't have to find an interpreter for every occasion. It all depends on the individual sermon or special occasion. The Deaf child needs the opportunity to interact with other Deaf children or Deaf adults of the same faith. Perhaps a discussion about relevant topics could take place at home, getting feedback from the child and answering questions about the event in question. You could show your child picture books of religious stories. You could seek out Deaf ministers, if there are any of your faith in the area, and always remember that some ministers sign. If these options are not feasible, invest in an interpreter, even if it does seem more convenient to avoid the whole issue.

How can parents ensure their Deaf child's right to access to information?

• Involve yourself in a Deaf Action Group. These groups help make public institutions recognize the need for information displays and TTYs in malls and other areas where pay phones are located, allowing the Deaf child more freedom and independence as well as more access to information.

• Make sure that your child has direct information from doctors and other professionals. Do not permit the information to be passed only between parents and the professional. If necessary bring an interpreter to doctors' (and other professional) appointments.

• Some religious groups – including Buddhist, Jewish, Protestant and Catholic denominations – have a full Deaf congregation. If your faith does not have a Deaf congregation, there may be a minister, rabbi, priest or other person who knows how to sign. Or you can expose your child to religion by hiring an interpreter to attend services or classes with your child.

CHAPTER EIGHT

TECHNOLOGY

As long as we have deaf people on earth,
we will have signs and as long as we have our film,
we can preserve our beautiful sign language
in its original purity.

George William Veditz, 1913

TECHNOLOGY

I N ORDER TO BE independent citizens, Deaf individuals
need to have full access to information that, in whole or
in part, affects our life. To fully achieve this, Deaf children must have access to, and be able to use, technology.
There are many recent and not-so-recent technological
advances that have made it possible for Deaf people to
access the same information as hearing people. Technology
has come a long way in eliminating many barriers and
thereby empowering Deaf people, children in particular, to
participate more meaningfully in everyday life. Closed-
caption decoders, TTYs, e-mail and flashing-light technology are all used to enable Deaf people to gain independence
in their daily lives.

A closed-caption decoder is a machine much like a
VCR that is attached to the television set; it provides subtitles of conversations and background noises for all kinds
of television programs – sports, news, movies and more.
Although closed-captioning is identified by a symbol on
videotapes or at the start of broadcast programs, viewers
will not see the subtitles without a decoder. As of 1994, all
new television sets manufactured in North America have

been required by law to be equipped with built-in decoders.

Let me tell you about an all-too-familiar scenario. Parents with an eight-year-old Deaf child have enrolled her in a school which follows a program based on the oral philosophy; that is, their daughter is expected to communicate through speech and lip-reading. This is a choice which does not encourage access to sign language or the opportunity to interact with other Deaf children who use ASL. When her parents are asked if a closed-caption decoder is in the home so that she can better understand television programs, they answer, "No. What's the point? This is a hearing world. It's a great opportunity for her to practice lip-reading."

Though well intentioned, this response reflects a sadly unrealistic expectation of their daughter. It is, in a sense, a form of punishment, for it forces her to practice "hearing." The parents have forgotten how hard Deaf children struggle to hear even the slightest sound, let alone the rapid and often hard-to-decipher conversations of the characters on TV. Surely this child has the right to learn and be entertained and informed without barriers, just as her hearing peers are.

Closed-caption decoders provide all children, hearing and Deaf, with access to English literacy as well as the enjoyment of TV programs. Their use promotes reading. It does not take away from children who want to lip-read. In situations where a speaker's face cannot be seen, the Deaf child can still read the speaker's words and understand what is happening. All children have accessibility rights. Decoders are a resource that grants children their rights.

A TTY (teletype machine) is attached to the phone enabling both parties to converse visually. The TTY has a small keyboard with a screen displaying the conversation typed. The switch of a button can also record the two-way conversation on paper, if the parties desire. The receiver and the transmitter of the telephone handset are placed on the acoustic coupler of the teletype machine and thus the message is relayed directly. Fortunately, some provincial governments in Canada provide financial support to those who require a TTY. Phone conversations are now possible even when one of the parties does not have a TTY. Using a relay service, operators equipped with a TTY and a voice phone relay messages in confidence between two parties. Finding one of these relay operators is often a simple matter of consulting the phone book or getting in touch with the local phone company.

Flashing-light technology, on the other hand, is designed to replace the sound environment. With this system in place, lights flash to indicate that someone is at the door, that the baby is crying, or that the fire alarm is ringing. The number of flashes signifies which of these events is occurring. Some alarm clocks use flashing lights instead of a bell or buzzer; others use vibrators.

Of course, getting the attention of Deaf children is not always a matter of special technology, especially if we remember how sensitive they are to visual cues. Flashing the lights off and on can also be effective – slow flashing to indicate the child is wanted; fast flashing to suggest a more urgent situation.

The astounding impact of the computer, and particularly the Internet, on lives of Deaf people is hard to measure. Mostly a silent form of communication, the technology allows everyone – hearing and Deaf – to carry on business, access information and record data equally.

Parents with Deaf children often ask, "Should we get a TTY, a decoder, and all this flashing-light technology? And if we do, should we wait until our child can read?"

JOANNE S. CRIPPS

The answer to the first question is a clear yes; the answer to the second is a decided no. If you are a parent in this situation, both you and your child will benefit from getting visual technology as early as possible. You will be able to communicate more easily with all Deaf people while your child will be more actively involved in everyday life, and therefore, less likely to tune out of the normal social interaction that hearing people take for granted. Your child can converse more meaningfully with family and friends about what is going on in his or her own life and the larger world. As a parent, you will feel more comfortable about your child's safety and sense of self-worth. I would suggest for the above reasons that access to this technology is not a privilege, but a right.

All types of technological equipment allow Deaf children to be more independent. However, Deaf children can better benefit from these resources and the access they provide if they have the opportunity to learn about Deaf history and Deaf role models, about the struggles and triumphs of their forerunners, about the development of sign language, and especially about controversial issues such as cochlear implants and the oral philosophy, not to mention other knowledge of the world needed to engage meaningfully in current events. This is not to say that we tell Deaf children exactly what we perceive as right or wrong, but rather we let them have full knowledge of the Deaf and hearing worlds. We should attempt to provide the information that will involve them fully in debates and let them decide on issues for themselves.

As parents of a Deaf child, how can you make technology work for your family?

- Acquire and learn how to use e-mail services

and the Internet, TTYs, flashing-light technology and other visual communicators for the home.

• Lobby for adoption of technology for Deaf people to gain access to information in schools and public places.

• Keep abreast of the latest technical products and services.

CHAPTER NINE

THE RIGHT TO PRIVACY

It takes an entire village to raise a child.

African proverb

THE RIGHT TO PRIVACY

RIVACY RIGHTS FOR Deaf children? But we have been giving them their privacy rights. They get to have their own rooms, don't they? How is it that we've been neglecting their privacy rights?

Our first reaction may be flat denial, but the truth is, in one way or another, we have been infringing on Deaf children's right to privacy. Perhaps the problem lies in our definition of "privacy" which, as our good friend the *Oxford Dictionary* tells us, has two meanings: "the state of being away from others, alone and undisturbed" and "secrecy as opposed to publicity." The first of these meanings is not too difficult to recognize; the second is too easy to ignore.

Let me give you an all too common scenario. A visitor enters a classroom where there are Deaf children, hoping to observe the daily activities and gain information that he or she can use as a parent or a teacher of a Deaf child at another school. The children being observed may be in a Deaf residential school, or perhaps they are in a hearing school, either separated in a self-contained classroom or integrated with their hearing classmates. A staff resource

101

person, acting in the admirable spirit of concern and help-fulness, guides the visitor, offering information about each student: this student has Deaf parents, that student had minimal language skills when he entered, and that other one is here in a special program designed to meet his behavioural needs. In the observation rooms of some schools, staff routinely refer to Deaf children's audiograms (a graph produced by a hearing test that determines the range of audible sounds heard by the individual) on dis-play, perhaps with their names visible, in order to explain how well the children are doing. The whole situation seems harmless enough – until we ask ourselves one very important question: would these resource or staff members so readily disclose such personal information if hearing children were involved?

Let's be clear on this point. During classroom tours, all students have the right to privacy about their background. Staff and other professionals must not divulge information to visitors or to student teachers about their pupils, even if this information appears to be harmless information about their parents, their reading or speaking abilities or even their degree of Deafness. They are there to see how educa-tion is carried on.

If these observers wish to know something about a cer-tain student, they should interview that student through an interpreter so that the student can decide whether to disclose this personal information. In doing so, we not only teach people how to communicate with Deaf children but also empower Deaf children to assert their right to determine what kind of information they feel comfortable sharing.

Article 16 of the United Nations Convention on the Rights of the Child, with regard to the Protection of Privacy, states, "The child has a right not to be subjected to arbitrary or unlawful interference with his or her privacy, family, home or correspondence, nor to unlawful attacks on his or her honour and reputation."

We face similar questions about confidentiality and privacy in regard to Deaf students' TTY conversations. Many people think nothing of reading printed TTY conversations or even of keeping them. If they are prepared to truly recognize a Deaf person's right to privacy, they should ask permission first. Deaf students do not have access to telephone voice conversations, but they should have the same right to privacy as hearing people when they talk on the phone. After all, bugging telephone communication is illegal without a warrant obtained by the police or other recognized authorities. Reading printed TTY conversations may not seem like illegally bugging a telephone or showing someone's private mail to another person, but at the very least it represents a form of unwelcome eavesdropping.

What may be required here is the same sort of system involved in the now widespread use of the Message Relay Service, which consists of operators who use voice and TTY at the same time. In Canada there are a few message relay services operated by local phone companies. The Message Relay Service and the Bell Relay Service provide a communication link between a TTY user and a telephone user. Before this service was available, Deaf people had to ask parents, siblings or even neighbours to make personal calls for them. Not only was this process inconvenient, but it also meant that they had to disclose personal information to those making the calls on their behalf. With the Message Relay Service, operators cannot and will not divulge what goes on in these telephone conversations, and there is a strict complaint procedure that the phone company rigorously adheres to.

JOANNE S. CRIPPS

An incident occurred where a Deaf boy with a hearing girlfriend called her through the Message Relay Service to discuss some very serious matters. Though these difficulties were just between them, the operator knew the boy's mother and let her in on the details. The boy was shocked, knowing full well that no one but the operator would know this information. He contacted the phone company manager, who investigated the matter and determined that there had indeed been a breach of trust. The operator was fired.

We must remember that Deaf children and adults who must use this vital service deserve to have their privacy rights respected. They should feel as sure about the confidentiality of their conversation as two hearing people would when talking to one another without a third person present.

Reading Deaf children's mail is yet another matter. Since written language is, in a very real sense, their second language, they may need help in reading their mail. In fact, many children are amazed and delighted at the wealth of information available through letters. However, we should all try to remember what we would feel like if someone began opening and reading our mail – especially without permission! If adults want to help children, they should ask if they can read the letter together and then explain what it means.

Now we need to consider the role of interpreters. First it must be understood that the Deaf community is small. Deaf people welcome others who are hearing into that community for language interaction and exposure. They reveal a lot about themselves: what they do, how they feel and who they are. They do so trusting that the information revealed is confidential, not necessarily meant for outsiders. Although interpreters are generally wonderful people, some may unintentionally invade Deaf people's privacy rights, particularly if children are involved – as if somehow the rules of confidentiality apply only to grownups.

In the second or third year of interpreter training, students sometimes visit law courts to observe how Deaf people use interpreters and how interpreters conduct themselves in the courtroom. Their professors or instructors argue that the students need exposure in order to discover how interpreting situations work and that, after all, courtrooms are public places. I agree, but before these students enter the courtroom, they must examine the relevance of this process from a perspective other than their own. They need to learn much more about the values of the Deaf community, to become more sensitive to issues that Deaf people find important, not the least of which is the need for privacy. True, these students need experience (sometimes years of it) to become fully qualified court interpreters, but they could learn just as much or more about interpreting situations through role playing in mock trials and then videotaping the results. Such a process would not only open a discussion of issues vital to the Deaf community but also make the entire observation process seem less like a visit to a zoo. A good interpreter will know when he or she is ready to take part in courtroom procedures and will seek a mentor for guidance. I once was in court to testify and was faced with four interpreters. It was an intimidating experience, with two interpreters on for fifteen minutes (the first one responsible for the voice interpretation and the second one responsible for my comments). Just as I was getting used to the process, the fifteen minutes were up and it was time to change interpreters. This went on for a day. I felt as if I was engulfed in bodyguards. The ideal situation would be to have just one interpreter.

It may be helpful to discuss how the general issue of privacy rights applies to one very specific and significant situation: reporting incidents of child abuse to the Children's Aid Society (CAS). If you ever have to report child abuse, here are a few suggestions to help ensure that the child will not feel at a disadvantage.

1. When reporting an incident to the Children's Aid Society, please inform the child step by step what you have done and are planning to do. Never assume that all children understand the role of the CAS. Bear in mind that some of them think of this institution as some sort of police system. Always explain, and make sure that children understand, the role and procedures of the CAS. If a social worker is involved, make it clear that the Society will provide a professional interpreter and/or Deaf interpreter.

2. If a child discloses an incident to you, ask if he or she wants an interpreter. Of course, the child may feel comfortable communicating to you without one. Fine! Don't assume that an interpreter is required in every case. However, if the meeting between you and the child also involves a hearing individual who does not understand sign language, or uses voice and sign at the same time, then an interpreter is required. In any case, you should check with the child to see if he or she is satisfied with the interpreter.

3. When leaving the room while the child is still there, always explain where you are going, even if you are simply going to make copies of documents or talk to someone else. It can be very troubling for Deaf children in this situation if they are not told of your whereabouts. They may think that you are talking about them behind their back.

While growing up, we all understood the value of privacy in our own lives. As parents, we must also understand the importance and value of privacy in our children's lives.

What can parents do to help ensure that their children have their privacy rights maintained?

- Make the children aware of private information. Let them understand what is personal versus public information; explain what can be kept to themselves and what can be shared and in what situations.

- Allow children to have private phone conversations and to read their own mail.

- Encourage children to be assertive when deciding what information they want to share about themselves.

CHAPTER TEN

EQUAL STANDARDS IN EDUCATION

When Tomorrow Comes...

And now here I stand
Looking out at...
Yet looking up to
The many people
Who've encouraged us
To follow our dreams.
You were the leaders of yesterday,
And still you lead today
Because we need you
But we know that
You want us to take the reins
Tomorrow.

Christine L. Steele

Christine was inspired to write this poem on the occasion of her graduation. She wanted to thank her teachers and her parents for believing in her and encouraging her to continue reaching for her goals and dreams. It reflects the widespread hope of those in the Deaf community that Christine and others will take their place in the community and work to make it a better place to live. Christine now teaches ASL and loves to travel.

EQUAL STANDARDS IN EDUCATION

RECENTLY, I WAS discussing various issues with several Deaf adults who attended hearing public schools. The two stories below are fairly typical of their educational experiences.

One adult recounted, "I felt different. It didn't matter how much help or support I got in the hearing school, I still felt different. I had to sit up in the front row or nearest to the front row. Even though I had some hearing, I missed out on a lot. I had to make friends with whoever was willing and was patient enough to explain almost everything for me. I wanted to run for President of Student Parliament. I had the potential but not the kind of leadership they wanted. Then I went to Gallaudet University. It was a whole new world for me. It was culture shock. I had to learn sign language and I was not prepared for the full participation that it gave me. For a long time, I was angry. I felt cheated of what I could have been when growing up."

Another adult had this to say about growing up: "All my life, I learned the oral method. It never seemed like a naturally acquired language for me. When I went to Gallaudet, I learned American Sign Language, but it still

111

didn't feel like an acquired language. It was as if I learned two different languages by memory and not through natural cultural interaction. Even now, I still experience this problem and am going through the emotionally bitter stages."

Both accounts demonstrate that the adults wished they had acquired ASL at an early age and had used it in their education. It would have allowed them to acquire language naturally through social interaction. When I asked them what method they should have used in the first place, they both replied, "American Sign Language. Speech is an option. We should have been able to decide which path we wanted to take." They felt they were missing information about residential schools and Deaf people. They did not feel they had been fully exposed to another option or way of life – one that might have been far better.

It may be hard for hearing people to understand the frustration and bitterness described in these accounts; after all, hearing people have full access to all the information presented in the classroom. Deaf students, in contrast, must be content with partial information, with what someone else has selected as the "important points." Meaningful learning for all students, including Deaf students, means having access to all the information conveyed and then deciding for themselves what is or is not useful. For Deaf students, the traditional oral approach should be merely an option, not the only method available. If Deaf students want to learn speech, they should have the opportunity. After school programs and enrichment programs may be suitable times for them to learn speech. What they need more than anything is exposure to natural sign language, a natural style of learning. This is their right.

Efficient classroom education means learning without

struggles or barriers. It means access to Deaf role models, such as teachers, principals, counsellors and guest speakers as well as information about historical and contemporary figures. It means full and equal participation in classroom discussion and debate, extracurricular activities, sports and school elections. Deaf students will learn best in a classroom full of other Deaf students, where well-trained staff understand Deaf norms and concerns and promote Deaf issues such as ASL literacy and social literacy, and provide access to culturally appropriate learning materials.

In a hearing-oriented environment, Deaf children are often expected to understand conversations, to participate in group discussions and to hear playmates behind, in front and all around them. It is often assumed that somehow Deaf people hear announcements over public address systems or on the radio; that they understand the quick and easy interaction of peers as they walk down the street; that they comprehend dinner-table conversations and debates; and that they know about the countless bits of information everyone else takes for granted. How easy it is to look at this picture from the outside, to see Deaf and hearing children mingling, perhaps playing together. It all seems so pleasant, positive and progressive. How easy it is to forget the stress imposed on Deaf children who have to deal with the assumption that they are being included and the expectation that they should be happy about it. This is not inclusion: it is exclusion.

Deaf children who are mainstreamed may grow up feeling that they are not part of a team. They may have an inner conflict or struggle concerning the question, How do I fit in? One student believed he would be hearing once he finished school in a mainstreamed setting. He felt he would understand all about hearing culture and norms once he graduated.

JOANNE S. CRIPPS

True inclusion means full participation, the ability to give and receive, to engage in friendly chit-chat or more meaningful debate. According to hearing norms, inclusion means putting the Deaf child in a group of hearing children to make things look normal and natural, the way things should be. By doing so, however, we are effectively isolating them. Of course, this does not mean that Deaf children should never mingle with their hearing friends and vice versa. Deaf children need a strong foundation as they begin their lives in our society; inclusion means providing them with nothing less than the best tools to make the most of their choices in life. With these tools and our support, Deaf children can decide their own destiny and not have their destiny decided for them.

Individualized programs help maintain the level of education desired by students and parents. It is imperative that each child and his or her educational setting be looked at independently. A child who is mainstreamed must be assessed on more than his or her apparent lip-reading skills. Reading the teacher's lips does not always tell a student everything that is happening in the classroom. Every child needs to gather information from other students and sources. Will this child be able to do this? Will the child be able to fully participate in all areas of development in the classroom just like every other child in the room? Can this child speak and be understood?

The same care and consideration must be given to a child placed in a Deaf residential setting. Even if some teachers know ASL, their degree of competence may vary, leading to a situation where the teachers do not fully understand what the children are signing and where the Deaf students end up teaching the teachers their language. True, both sides may learn something from this situation; however, if the burden of complete communication falls on the shoulders of the Deaf child, the educational system is not doing its job.

The burden of assumptions and expectations of hearing individuals is even heavier for Deaf children who speak well. Many people believe that a student who can speak can also hear. Sometimes, this assumption may lead to a situation where school staff may refuse to believe that a student is truly Deaf. They may describe the individual as "manipulative" or "controlling," and "always wanting her own way" or "hearing only what he wants to hear." In some cases, they actually set up various situations to test the child's hearing. They may also believe that the child can understand English well, and thus, can read and write without difficulty. This is not necessarily true. Students still need input through their natural language.

Deaf students require a classroom environment where they can develop linguistic, mathematical and artistic skills in ASL, their natural language. It should go without saying that these children cannot acquire these skills with a teacher who is not trained in ASL, and who therefore does not understand the student's mother tongue. The solution to this problem does not mean bringing in a Deaf teacher to cater to one particular Deaf student. To interact naturally in and out of the classroom, a Deaf child needs contact with as many Deaf adults and children as possible, not only to ensure an education comparable to that of hearing children but also to acquire a language and become exposed to Deaf culture.

Providing an ideal educational environment for Deaf students is not easy, but one approach has recently proved both popular and successful: the Bilingual-Bicultural Program. This child-centred system helps students to develop in both ASL and English; to understand and appreciate Deaf culture; and, during this process, to foster the positive self-image needed to function successfully in both the Deaf and hearing worlds.

There is a lot of research supporting these findings. The recent research of Dave Mason, Ph.D. shows that the use of ASL in activities such as discussions does help Deaf readers improve their reading and writing skills.*

To understand what this program involves, we first need to understand what is meant by the terms bilingual and bicultural. Since Deaf children lack full and unhindered access to spoken language, they do not learn English through a natural process. Thus, the central principle of the bilingual approach to Deaf education is that ASL is the most accessible language for Deaf children simply because it is acquired naturally. Not surprisingly in such a program, teachers and students use ASL both in and out of the classroom. However, as the word bilingual suggests, students also develop skills in English through the usual activities related to literacy: reading and writing. Of course, those students who would benefit from developing their speech and auditory potential receive the appropriate training.

The notion of biculturalism for Deaf students entails more than simply fostering the understanding and respect necessary for Deaf students to function in both worlds. In fact, the bicultural approach encourages and empowers students to appreciate and take pride in the language and literature, the history and heritage, the values and verities of Deaf people.

Schools that adopt this approach incorporate bilingual and bicultural principles into every aspect of their curriculum. In doing so, they maximize the opportunities for Deaf children to develop their cognitive and linguistic skills

* Dave Mason is a Deaf professor at York University, Toronto. His findings will be presented at the next World Federation of the Deaf Congress.

and thus allow them to lead full academic and social lives. Through interaction with a variety of Deaf and hearing people, students can be fully participating and contributing members of both environments. "But full literacy implies far more than basic reading and writing proficiency. It implies an enculturation into ways of thinking, interpreting, and using language in a variety of complex activities and settings, typical of a rapidly changing and technologically advanced society."*

To achieve these goals, a bilingual-bicultural education must be child-centred; in other words, it must recognize that Deaf children come from a variety of backgrounds. The majority of Deaf children have hearing parents who are not completely proficient in ASL or lack access to information about Deaf education. Some of these children are born Deaf; others become Deaf at a later age, either before or after acquiring some auditory language skills. Furthermore, some students do not use English at home. In response to this diversity, the bilingual-bicultural approach uses the Individualized Education Plan (IEP) to help assess each child's abilities to determine what needs to be provided that would prove beneficial.

Another vital tenet of the bilingual-bicultural approach is that students' progress in another language depends on developing a strong base in a first language. As in any other school system, children are introduced to various reading and writing tasks as their skills develop. However, their proficiency in English is assessed not simply by their ability to read lips and to speak, but also by their ability to read and write in English. In order to encourage discussion and exchange of information, the bilingual-bicultural school provides ASL storytelling and

* Technical Report No. 1, The Literacies Institute: Its Mission, Activities and Perspective on Literacy (September 1989, Newton, MA).

videotapes, encourages conversational dialogue with models of ASL and English, offers a variety of books, other printed material and videotaping technology, and ensures access to computers in all grades.

By far the most important principle of the bilingual-bicultural approach is the commitment to nurturing Deaf children's self image. By studying Deaf history and culture and by being exposed to a range of Deaf role models, Deaf students can take pride in being members of a unique linguistic and cultural group while also learning to understand and accept the many other cultural groups in their country and beyond.

Articles 28 and 29 of the United Nations Convention on the Rights of the Child state that, "... education is directed at developing the child's personality and talents; preparing the child for responsible life in a free society; and developing respect for the child's parents, basic human rights, the natural environment and the child's own cultural and national values and those of others."

The bilingual-bicultural approach recognizes that the home environment significantly affects a child's growing sense of self. As a result, this approach provides support and training for parents, siblings and members of the extended family so that they will gain the skills and knowledge necessary to promote mutual understanding and strengthen the family bond.

A practice now employed by Deaf residential schools in deciding whether to admit students into their program is to find out the degree of their hearing loss. In Ontario, the Board schools will maintain that if the hearing loss is less than 70 decibels, it will provide a program in the mainstream school and not send the child to a Deaf school. If a child does not have a 70 decibel hearing loss, he or she is not considered Deaf enough to attend a provincial school for the Deaf in Ontario. This type of ruling is arbitrary. Instead, we should look at the child and see what his or her needs are, regardless of measured hearing loss. If a child with some hearing attends a school for the Deaf, that child is still entitled to and can enjoy the same rights as everyone else, in that he or she can learn to be bilingual in ASL and written English. If decibel loss is used as the deciding factor for admittance to a Deaf school, do we not take away the child's right to choose? A child might thrive in a bilingual-bicultural environment and perhaps needs this environment all the more. It is very easy for us to say, Sorry, you have too much hearing, you can't stay here. This implies that the child is neither Deaf nor hearing and therefore belongs to no world.

During a presentation I gave on cross-cultural mediation at a university, I posed one question to the whole group: A child is seven years old and has some hearing. Where do you feel this child should go: to a Deaf school or a hearing school? Right away, I was bombarded with questions asking what his parents were like. Could they sign? Do they use voice only? It pained me to see that the audience was forming their decision based on the outside sphere of this child. Not one question was asked to see whether this child had rights to access and/or a need to be in a Deaf environment.

One of the parents at the presentation informed me that it took them three years to get their daughter into a Deaf residential school. The child could hear quite well, could talk to her parents over the phone, could hear conversations going on around her, but she was still Deaf. She had had a lot of problems in the hearing school she was attending. Still, the authorities would not enroll her in the Deaf school because of her hearing. The parents knew their rights and resolved to fight their way in. Finally they got their daughter enrolled. Within four months, she was thriving. Her parents are very pleased with her progress.

So, what do we do about this situation? Change everything to make Deaf children happy? No, not at all. But we need to grant Deaf children their right to interact with other Deaf children and to enjoy the same access as hearing children.

Hearing children can hear the teacher, hear questions asked in the classroom, hear and participate in discussions, hear the voice on films and videos, hear announcements on the public address system, hear the guide on field trips, hear their friends chatting during lunch and recess, hear speakers during assemblies, etc. How do we ensure that Deaf children gain access to the best education for them? The answer is clear. Deaf children need a lot of visual exposure and access. When you are looking at schools and considering schooling options, ask yourself the following questions.

- Does this school promote the necessary parts for empowering education for Deaf children (e.g. cultural and linguistic incorporation, community participation, interactive pedagogy and advocacy-oriented evaluation)? (See Appendix for more information.)

- Would it be to your child's educational, social and emotional advantage to be taught in the Deaf environment?

- Will your child's social and emotional needs be met? Will he or she be given the opportunity to communicate comfortably and to develop language skills naturally? Will he or she have the opportunity to exercise their leadership abilities and develop their own personalities while receiving an education that will allow them to function among both Deaf and hearing people?

• Does your school promote after school activities to increase ASL literacy skills, e.g. sports, dances, and tournaments?

• Not all mainstream programs can provide the same services. What exactly happens in the mainstream program you are considering?

• Will your child be placed in a regular class with hearing students and taught by a teacher with no special training in the education of Deaf children? If so, will efforts be made to ensure your child gets Deaf cultural experiences in other parts of their lives, e.g. Deaf Camps, Mayfest, Deaf community events?

• Does this school have qualified sign language interpreting services?

• Are teachers and support staff knowledgeable about Deaf issues? Do they keep abreast of current events? Do they promote linguistic development in their native language? Are teachers well trained in terms of ASL literacy and written literacy development?

• Will your child be exposed to Deaf teachers and other Deaf adults or will your child have only hearing adults as role models? Will your

JOANNE S. CRIPPS

child be given opportunities to see Deaf role models so that he or she can begin to imagine what the future could hold?

• Does this school promote equal access: a TTY for each phone; visual technology such as flashing lights for fire alarm, door bell and phone ringing; open captioned TVs on public address system; and TVs equipped with closed captioned decoders? *

---

* Information on pages 120 - 121 is adapted from "You and Your Deaf Child: Information Sharing Kit for Parents" (Toronto: Ontario Association of the Deaf and Ontario Cultural Society of the Deaf, 2000 rev.)

CHAPTER ELEVEN

JUSTICE AND SOCIAL ACCOUNTABILITY

Our deepest fear is NOT that we are inadequate.
Our deepest fear is that we are powerful beyond measure.
It is our light, not our darkness that most frightens us.
We ask ourselves,
Who am I to be brilliant, gorgeous, talented and fabulous?
Actually, who are you not to be?...
It is not just in some of us. It is in everyone.
And as we let our own light shine,
we unconsciously give other people permission
to do the same.
As we are liberated from our own fear,
our presence automatically liberates others.

Nelson Mandela, 1994 Inaugural Speech

JUSTICE AND SOCIAL ACCOUNTABILITY

CHILDREN WHO DO not learn the meaning of active citizen engagement may become uninterested and apathetic adults. Such attitudes can lead to a neglect of the rights and privileges found in a democracy. Informed and active citizens are important at the local, provincial, national and international levels. All of these realities apply even more clearly to those who are Deaf.

Deaf citizens need to bring awareness of Deaf issues to the forefront and use the available laws to combat discrimination, systemic barriers and violations of rights. We must take responsibility but in order to do this, we must understand our position before the law. We need the knowledge, skills, understanding and attitudes necessary to function in a society based on the rule of law. Effective standards relevant to education in the law include classroom use of outside resource persons, including Deaf mentors; appropriate case materials; teaching strategies that foster true student interaction; the involvement of important school administrators; and professional peer support for teachers. These strategies have proven effective in motivating students to learn and to exercise their civic responsibilities.

What are the results of an inadequate understanding of our legal rights? Perhaps we should consider the following situation. A Deaf person was arrested for vandalizing another person's car. While in court, his lawyer asked the police officer if he had read the client his rights. The officer said no, and when asked why, said, "Well, I cannot sign to him." The lawyer went on to point out that, by law, the officer must read his client's rights to him before the arrest and he could do so by obtaining the services of an interpreter. Because of this simple oversight, the case was dismissed. This result helps no one. The individual, if guilty, evades accountability. If not guilty, then he has to depend on the alertness of his lawyer to avoid being charged for a crime that he did not commit.

A Deaf mother expecting a baby took prenatal classes when there were no fully qualified interpreters. The instructor of the course claimed to have the ability to sign (often people who take one ASL class feel they are able to communicate through sign), so the situation, though not ideal, was better than nothing. When she went into labour and arrived at the hospital operating room, her doctor was there, along with three nurses and about fifteen interns observing the birth. The woman felt embarrassed and she was unsure why all the people were there. She used gestures to ask her doctor who simply patted her hand and advised her not to worry.

Now, if this mother had taken a course in law and understood her rights, she would have known what to do; in fact, she might have even filed a complaint. But, of course, not knowing her rights, she did not. When asked why she had not done something about it sooner, she said, "Well, I didn't know. I felt so embarrassed to have them watching me deliver my baby and I wasn't able to get my message across. I didn't know my rights. I was afraid if I complained, they would think I was stupid."

So, the question here is simple: how can we help Deaf children understand the law well enough not only to change the political system but also to recognize their own accountability?

Schools, especially those that offer law-related courses, have a responsibility to adapt or, even better, develop from scratch a curriculum designed for Deaf students. This curriculum should include the names of Deaf politicians, lawyers and advocates as well as other professionals as resources. This is the only way issues of legal rights and responsibilities can become clear to Deaf students.

A curriculum designed by the Deaf should include brainstorming, cooperative learning, small-group participation, the use of resource people, case study methods, mock trials, group and individual presentations, peer teaching, discussion of controversial issues, the development of critical thinking and discussion skills, and the opportunity for expressing and defending opinions. All these things require a lot of in-depth planning and lots of hands-on experience. As matters now stand, Deaf students often receive what amounts to censored information, largely due to varying reading and language levels as well as to different social norms and the ASL language skills of the teacher.

Educating students about their rights and responsibilities will lead to productive membership in both the Deaf and hearing communities. We must provide this knowledge and training to prepare Deaf children and youth for a world of opportunity. Only then will they become informed, participating citizens.

As parents, you can help your Deaf child learn about the laws that directly affect him or her. If the school your child is attending does not offer a law course that incorporates Deaf rights and responsibilities, make sure you speak to the teachers and principal of the school to discuss how the situation can be remedied.

Being informed of their legal rights is essential for Deaf children, but claiming these rights will mean little if they are not prepared to fulfill their legal responsibilities. Let's consider a scenario similar to those mentioned above, but this time involving a Deaf youth on probation who is caught breaking the law. The police interview him through a professional interpreter who advises the youth that, under normal circumstances, he would be charged, but that this charge will be waived because the relevant corrections facility does not provide Deaf services.

Now, wait a minute. Let's step back and look at what's going on here. Are we saying that, just because there are no Deaf services available, some Deaf juveniles accused of crimes get off without being charged? Shouldn't they be held accountable for their actions? Doesn't the corrections facility have a responsibility to set up a Deaf unit, even though it may serve relatively few individuals? What about the accountability of those young people to the law? What about the justice system itself? How can we ensure that each Deaf youth receives justice equal to that received by other juveniles? Let me answer these questions as clearly and emphatically as I can.

First of all, when Deaf young people break the law, they are accountable for their actions. However, we can ensure that they enjoy the same rights and safeguards as any other young offenders in the same situation. Some people have argued that ensuring these rights means handing out special privileges. Not so! Once again, these people are confusing rights with privileges. The reality is that Deaf children are twice punished if we fail to recognize their rights. If, for example, a hearing young offender in a corrections facility enjoys the privilege of watching television for two hours, we are not accommodating a Deaf young person's rights by simply giving him or her more viewing time. The Deaf youth should receive the same amount of time, but have a closed-caption decoder attached to the set. This too is not a special privilege, but a basic right.

Furthermore, we must educate Deaf clients about their rights in the legal system so they not only know quite clearly what they are legally entitled to do and not do, but also understand their responsibility to speak up for themselves and not let lawyers make assumptions or speak on their behalf without consultation on the basic issues. As things now stand, Deaf people are too often excluded from the legal process simply because finding a competent interpreter, especially a Deaf interpreter, is time consuming or because no one has determined who is going to pay for these services. However, having access to a "trained" interpreter does not always ensure perfect communication. What sometimes happens is that a monolingual Deaf client may not understand an interpreter for whom ASL is a second language. This client needs a Deaf interpreter who can explain legal matters in the child's first or native language – ASL.

What can parents do to ensure that their Deaf child is a responsible citizen who is socially accountable and knows how the justice system works?

- Encourage your child to learn as much about the law and about his or her rights and responsibilities as he or she can.

- If a law course incorporating instruction on how the law pertains to Deaf people does not

exist in your child's school, get support to inte-
grate such a course into the curriculum. A good
example to include is the Access for Deaf
Americans videotape. It highlights the rights
and responsibilities of Deaf people under the
Americans with Disabilities Act (1990).* It is a
valuable tool for both individual study and
group settings such as workshops and class-
rooms.

* Deaf groups in Ontario are campaigning for the Ontarians with Disabilities Act
(ODA) to be passed. For more information, visit www.indie.ca/oda

CHAPTER TWELVE

THE FUTURE

Canada Geese with determined grace,
Pass by in a V-line race.
As a leader tires and slows the pace,
Another emerges to take their place.
So like the Deaf in life give chase,
The outcome is a triumph.

Adapted by Joanne Cripps

This poem was written for the Signature Quilt to raise funds for the Canadian Deaf Festival 1998. It was inspired by the story "Goose Sense" from an out-of-print book called *High Flying Geese*, author unknown.

THE FUTURE

WHEN WE THINK ABOUT our children's future, particularly their career opportunities, we normally conjure up visions of school teachers, nurses, doctors and lawyers, to name only a few. Most high schools, colleges and universities hold career days in order to give interested students some idea of workplace realities. I have no objection to such events – or to such visions. But what about Deaf children? Where do they get their exposure to the working world? What or who is available to tell them about the working life, about the vast opportunities in the job market?

Perhaps it seems too early to worry about your child's career. It's not, especially if your son or daughter is Deaf. Employment options are not limited; they are virtually endless. Deaf people make excellent employees and excellent employers. For that reason alone, career days should include Deaf mentors and Deaf employees or employers wherever possible. There are Deaf lab technicians, lawyers, teachers, entrepreneurs, interpreters, chemists, ASL instructors, graphic artists, plumbers, ministers, authors, computer analysts and programmers – the list goes

133

on. We must never forget that Deaf children will grow up to be Deaf adults – adults entitled to all that the working world can offer.

Unfortunately, the law sometimes restricts what Deaf people can do for a living. In most jurisdictions, for example, bus drivers have to be hearing in order to ensure communication with their passengers as well as for safety. But what happens if the bus is full of Deaf students and the driver is a non-signing hearing person? The answer is simple: they can't communicate. What we need to do is to look at what is appropriate for the specific situation.

Let me offer a personal example, this one from my experience with Early Childhood Education. Wanting to earn a diploma in this field, I took a few courses, only to be advised by the administration that I would receive only a letter of standing. When asked why I would not receive a diploma like the others who had completed the same courses, administrators replied that, in a curriculum designed for hearing students, I would be unable to communicate. However, if I wanted to teach Deaf children, who are defined as "special needs" students, I would require another year of study to obtain my diploma.

I see things quite differently. I understand Deaf culture; I have the language needed to communicate with Deaf students. In short, I believe that I would provide them with a good role model. We should bear in mind that Deaf people don't see themselves as people with special needs. When a hearing person comes into a room filled with Deaf people, does this define her as a "special needs" person? The reality is that all children have similar expectations about social development, an integral part of which is the need for appropriate role models.

Perhaps Early Childhood Education needs to branch out into a two-tiered system. If hearing people wish to work with Deaf children, they have to take classes in ASL, ASL literacy and Deaf culture in addition to their regular curriculum. If Deaf people wish to work with hearing children, they can continue to take courses appropriate for this group.

Nowadays, everyone seems to be demanding rights, and even the apparently simple issues become controversial. Such is certainly the case with the concept of rights for Deaf children. However, we need to get back to the bottom line. What are Deaf children's rights and how do we ensure that they are recognized and exercised? As Deaf and hearing allies, we can cooperate to bring about a broader idea of "we" whereby both communities can benefit from each other's strengths. Deaf and hearing parents, lay people and professionals, the Deaf community and all their allies – all of us can link our strengths into a bridge of support for Deaf children as they grow up to realize their full potential.

As a fitting end to this book, I offer the following personal story by Audrey Byrne, mother of a Deaf son. The story itself refers primarily to her choice of a school for Deaf children, but it also speaks simply but eloquently of issues other than education, issues vital to the fair and informed consideration of Deaf children's rights.

Will They Understand?
By Audrey Byrne

As the mother of a child who is Deaf, I cannot count how often I have had to defend my decision to place him in a "segregated" setting (i.e. a school for Deaf children). It is interesting that the people who do not know anything about being Deaf are the ones who most often question my decision.

JOANNE S. CRIPPS

I put quotation marks around the word segregated because I never use that word when I describe my son and his educational setting. Those who most often question why I am segregating my son are the hearing people within the disability movement, professionals and parents alike, who advocate mainstreaming.

My son attends a school for the Deaf. His stepfather is Deaf. His friends are Deaf. Some of his teachers are Deaf. His vice-principal is Deaf. His family uses sign language. In short, he is included. He is part of his community: the Deaf community. He is not isolated.

I strongly believe that my son is in the best, least restrictive environment for him – an environment that provides him with free-flowing communication.

Let's suppose I followed the mainstream and placed him in an integrated setting in our neighbourhood school along with his twin sister, who happens to be hearing. He may, though this is not guaranteed, be provided with an aide who may, also not guaranteed, know some sign language but who will likely not be a certified interpreter or understand very much about Deaf culture. The aide, and probably far too many others, will rely on my son's sister to act as his interpreter. That is not her role in our family. I am not describing a worst-case scenario. I am describing a reality. I am describing what most commonly happens when parents do not have access to up-to-date, best-practice information about the proper education for their Deaf children. I am describing what happens when parents are given advice by professionals who ignore the recommendations of the Deaf community as to what is most advantageous for a Deaf child. This happens all across North America. I know this based on reading countless articles, research papers, reports and books, on listening to Deaf people's life stories, and on speaking with people across the country who work and live within the Deaf community.

It would be nice if we lived in a world that was truly inclusive, a world where everyone knew a common language and respected diverse cultures. But that is not reality.

I often struggle when asked about my decision for my son, the informed choice I made for my child. I often wonder whether they truly will understand the word segregated for my son in reality means full inclusion. His "disability" is actually a communication barrier to those who do not know his language. Ask Deaf adults if they are disabled and most will say no. The label of disability is placed on Deaf people by hearing folks. I never considered myself a "hearing" person until my son was born. Now I too wear a label: hearie. I too experienced isolation during the beginning of my journey while coming to understand my son and learn his language. I would feel isolated in a group of Deafies. I was the one with the disability. I know what my son experiences when people are not comfortable with him because they cannot communicate.

I am married to a Deaf man. Whenever we are out together and are signing, I do not use my voice. I know that salespeople, waiters and other service people are reluctant to approach us because they don't have a clue about how they can serve us. It is interesting to watch the expressions on their faces when they struggle to communicate. Not one ever considers grabbing a pen and communicating through the written word. They realize that I am not Deaf when I start to speak, and their expression is of one who has just seen a ghost. I still recall the police officer who stopped me and assumed I was Deaf because I had signed to my passenger to ask for the car registration in the glove compartment. The officer, assuming I read lips, then told me he knew that Deaf people could read lips very well. I then told him that, yes, a small percentage of Deaf people can read lips well enough to understand what he had just said, but I couldn't because I am hearing and have not taken years and years of speech therapy! He did not see the humour in what I had said and gave me a ticket. I guess every once in a while, even a mom can get a bit tired of educating everyone, even though I know that it is the only way to change attitudes and clear up misconceptions.

When I first started working for an organization that advocated for families of children with disabilities, it was a daily struggle to explain my choice for my son. You see, all of the staff advocate for inclusion and mainstreaming but, to different people, these terms have different meanings. To most people, inclusion means being part of their community, the place where their home stands, not a cultural-linguistic community that may be many miles away from the family home.

Some people may not find it acceptable to have community that is physically far away; others, like me, are glad that such a community exists at all! It means that I can access what is best for my child. I travel willingly. It is an informed choice I've made for my son. He is a Deaf child born into a hearing family, although when he was eight, I married his Deaf step-father and they share an incredible bond. He is integrated every day, at home and in school. I also advocate strongly on behalf of respecting the decisions made by parents. They may choose their neighbourhood as the community for their child or their choice may be similar to ours. All I ask is that their choice be an informed one.

I went through an interesting process along with the people I worked with on Deaf advocacy – one that involved listening to each other until we realized that what we were talking about was choice, not just any choice, but an informed one. We were then able to work side by side, driven by the belief that families should have choices and need access to information that will inform these choices.

Joanne S. Cripps

Some of my volunteer time has been spent on communities representing and promoting the rights of families who have Deaf sons and daughters. Time and energy are always willingly spent convincing people that it is vital to ensure and preserve the family's right to choose a segregated setting and not be penalized for their choice.

It is difficult for any family when faced with a decision that they never thought they would have to make. The difficulty increases when a family is made to feel guilty if they haven't made the right decision. We must respect each other's choices and, more importantly, understand that there is no one single best choice for all families. Individual situations must be considered.

I do not like the self-doubt that creeps in whenever I have made a decision, and I am still amazed that this happens because I know I have made the best choice for my child. He is happy and well adjusted. It is not fair to feel occasional doubts, but when I begin to consider once again the reasons for my decision, the self-doubt disappears and I feel proud that I have chosen well for my son.

I only ask that people respect a family's decision for their sons and daughters. No family should live their life wondering whether people will understand.

QUIET JOURNEY

It is true there are no clear laws protecting the rights of Deaf children. So this leaves a wide field of action for professionals, organizations and doctors with little knowledge (and in some cases biased opinions) about Deaf resources. William C. Stoke wrote, "The study of sign language of the deaf has two chief ends: to gain knowledge about what language is, and to help forward the education of deaf people." This quote comes from a book called *Seeing Language in Sign: The Work of William C. Stokoe* by Jane Maher with a foreword by Oliver Sacks. Stokoe, at that time an English literature professor, was the one who, in the 1960s, identified that ASL is a language. This book traces the process that Stokoe followed to prove scientifically and unequivocally that American Sign Language met the full criteria of linguistics.

We all have a moral responsibility. Rights are accorded on moral grounds. Rights should never be used as privileges. We all know that children have the right to be able to communicate. We would not dream of denying them this right. Yet, you and I, as parents, are faced with options and decisions on how to communicate with Deaf children. We see communication as a method for Deaf children when in fact it is not. I was once a Deaf child, now I'm a Deaf adult and parent. I've been there.

Look upon this as a journey. Be a parent to your child. Enjoy the benefits of being able to communicate in two languages or more. Learn the other side of the Deaf world. Remember, there is sunshine in the shadows.* Understanding the rights of your Deaf child allows you to be a true parent.

---

* Albernon Talmage, from *Helen McNicoll (1879-1915): A Canadian Impressionist* by Natalie Luckyj (Toronto: Art Gallery of Ontario, 1999).

APPENDIX

Please note that addresses and telephone numbers below are the main contacts. You can contact them and ask for your local organization, your faith association or a service agency for your area. If you do not have a TTY, you can call the Relay Service at 1-800-855-0511 and give your operator the TTY number requested.

INTERNATIONAL ORGANIZATIONS

The World Federation of the Deaf
Magnus Ladulasgatan 63-4tr   11 8 27 Stockholm   SWEDEN
Fax: 46 8 4421499   E-mail: info@wfdnews.org
Web site: www.wfdnews.org

World Deaf Games (CISS)
5/42 Wright Street   McKinnon, VIC 3204   AUSTRALIA
Fax: 61 3 9576 7924   E-mail: Lovett@ciss.org
Web site: www.ciss.org

CANADIAN NATIONAL DEAF ORGANIZATIONS

Canadian Association of the Deaf
251 Bank Street, Unit 203   Ottawa, ON   K2P
TTY: (613) 565-2882   V: (613) 565-2882
Fax: (613) 565-1207   E-mail: cad@cad.ca
Web site: www.cad.ca

Canadian Cultural Society of the Deaf
House 144, 11337 61 Avenue   Edmonton, AB   T6H 1M3
TTY: (403) 436-2599
Fax: (403) 430-9489   E-mail: ccsd@connect.ab.ca
Web site: www.ccsdeaf.com

Joanne S. Cripps

Canadian Deaf Sports Association c/o Ghysline Fiset
4545 Ave. Pierre-de-Coubertin CP 1000 Succ. M
Montreal, QC H1V 3R2
TTY: (514) 252-3069   Fax: (514) 251-8038
E-mail: assq@loisirquebec.qc.ca OR Gigifiset@loisirquebec.qc.ca
Web site: www.loisirquebec.qc.ca

Provincial Deaf Organizations

BRITISH COLUMBIA

B.C. Cultural Society of the Deaf
American Sign Language and Deaf Studies - King Edward Campus
1155 East Broadway Vancouver, BC V5N 5T9
TTY: (604) 871-7444
Fax: (604) 871-7442   E-mail: jwarren@vcc.bc.ca

Deaf Children's Society of B.C.
7355 Canada Way Burnaby, BC V3N 4Z6
TTY: (604) 525-9390   V: (604) 525-6056
Fax: (604) 525-7307   E-mail: deafchildren@infomatch.com
Web site: www.deafchildren.bc.ca

ALBERTA

Alberta Association of the Deaf
House #144, 11337 61 Avenue Edmonton, AB T6H 1M3
TTY: (780) 439-1822
Fax: (780) 430-9489   E-mail: mccarthy@icrossroads.com
Web site: www.connect.ab.ca/~aad

Alberta Cultural Society of the Deaf
House #144, 11337 61 Avenue Edmonton, AB T6H 1M3
TTY: (780) 456-9015

Alberta Deaf Sports Association
House #143, 11337 61 Avenue Edmonton, AB T6H 1M3
TTY: (780) 438-8079   V: (780) 438-8079
Fax: (780) 438-9114   E-mail: adsa@compusmart.ab.ca
Web site: www.compusmart.ab.ca/gu/adsa/ADSA.htm

SASKATCHEWAN

Saskatchewan Deaf Children's Society, Inc.
2209 Ewart Avenue   Saskatoon, SK S7J 1Y1
TTY: (306) 343-9611   V: (306) 343-9611

Saskatchewan Cultural Society of the Deaf
511 Main Street East   Saskatoon, SK S7N 0C2

Saskatchewan Deaf Sports Association
1860 Lorne Street   Regina, SK S4P 2L7
TTY: (306) 545-4440
Fax: (306) 924-1421   E-mail: lbirley@cableregina.com
kennethd@sk.sympatico.ca

MANITOBA

Deaf Centre Manitoba
285 Pembina Highway, 301   Winnipeg, MB R3L 2E1
TTY: (204) 284-7373   Fax: (204) 897-1961

ONTARIO

Ontario Literacy for Deaf People (GOLD)
150 Central Park Drive, Suite 106   Brampton, ON L9T 2T9
TTY: (905) 458-0499   V: (905) 458-0286
Fax: (905) 458-9348
Web site: www.deafcanada.com./GOLD/

Ontario Association of the Deaf
271 Spadina Road   Toronto, ON M5R 2V3
TTY: (416) 513-1893 & (416) 513-1894   V: (416) 413-0944
Fax: (416) 413-4822   E-mail: oad@globalserve.net
Web site: www.deafontario.org

Ontario Camp of the Deaf
2395 Bayview Ave   North York, ON M2L 1A2
TTY: (705) 378-0512   V: (705) 436-4813
Fax: (705) 436-4813 & (705) 378-0380 (summer)
E-mail: deafcamp@zeuter.com

Ontario Cultural Society of the Deaf
255 Ontario Street South, House #4   Milton, ON   L9T 2M5
TTY: (905) 878-6470   Fax: (905) 878-3752

Ontario Deaf Sports Association
255 Ontario Street South, House #4   Milton, ON   L9T 2M5
TTY: (905) 875-0723   Fax: (905) 875-0569
E-mail: office@ontariodeafsports.on.ca
Web site: www.ontariodeafsports.on.ca

Parents of Deaf-Plus Ontarians (PODPO)
570 Hood Road, Suite 15   Markham, ON   L3R 4G7
TTY: (905) 473-6525   V: (905) 485-0514
Fax: (905) 470-6484   E-mail: admin@podpo.org
Web site: www.podpo.org

QUEBEC

Société Culturelle Québécoise des Sourds
5515 Queen Mary West, Suite 101   Montreal, QC   H3X 1V4
TTY/Fax: (514) 482-6050   E-mail: aslm@total.net

Metropolitan-Montreal Deaf Community Centre
65 rue de Castelnau   Suite 300   Montreal, QC   H2R 2W3
TTY/V: (514) 279-7609   Fax: (514) 279-5373

NEW BRUNSWICK

Moncton Association of the Deaf
31 Garland Drive   Riverview, NB   E1B 3V3
TTY: (506) 386-8091

New Brunswick Deaf Sports Association
902-656 Brunswick Dr.   Saint John, NB   E2L 3S5

NOVA SCOTIA

Deafness Advocacy Association Nova Scotia
1660 Hollis Street, Suite 803   Halifax, NS   B3J 1V7
TTY: (902) 425-0119   V: (902) 425-0240
Fax: (902) 429-9312   E-mail: daans@ns.sympatico.ca

Eastern Canada Association of the Deaf
27 Elmwood Drive   Amherst, NS B4H 2H2
TTY/V: (902) 667-7142

Maritimes Cultural Society of the Deaf
1249 Queen Street, Apt. 304   Halifax, NS B3J 2H3
E-mail: mcdermjj@halifax.nscc.ns.ca

NEWFOUNDLAND

Newfoundland & Labrador Association of the Deaf
P.O. Box 21313   St. John's, NF A1A 5G6
TTY: (709) 576-4908   V: (709) 576-4592
Fax: (709) 576-7501

Newfoundland Deaf Sports Association c/o Brian Johnson
P.O. Box 21313   St. John's, NF A1A 5G6
TTY: (709) 364-2708   Fax: (709) 576-7501

INTERPRETER ASSOCIATIONS AND SERVICES

Association of Visual Language Interpreters of Canada
Canadian Evaluation System Office   11337-61 Avenue
Edmonton, AB T6H 1M3   TTY/V: (780) 430-9442
Fax: (780) 430-9489   E-mail: avlicces@freenet.edmonton.ab.ca

Prince George Interpreters Association
8113 Princeton Crescent   Prince George, BC V2N 3V6
V: (250) 964-3849
Fax: (250) 563-2612   E-mail: lister_chen@bc.sympatico.ca

Alberta Chapter of Registry of Interpreters for the Deaf
House #144, 11337-61 Avenue   Edmonton, AB T6J 5P9
V: (780) 438-2319
Fax: (780) 431-0831   E-mail: korpiniskid@inifinity.gmcc.ab.ca

Saskatchewan Association of Visual Language Interpreters
4180 Princess Street   Regina, SK S4S 3N3
V: (306) 584-8156
Fax: (306) 585-2582   E-mail: lizwarren@hotmail.com

JOANNE S. CRIPPS

Manitoba Association of Visual Language Interpreters
P.O. Box 22031, 1-120 Donald Street   Winnipeg, MB R3C 4G2
V: (204) 488-9486   Fax: (204) 452-0688

Ontario Association of Sign Language Interpreters
House #4, 255 Ontario Street South   Milton, ON L9T 2M5
TTY/V: (905) 639-9611
Fax: (416) 742-4223   E-mail: oasli@ican.net

Association québécoise des interpretes francophones en langage
visuel -AQIFLV
Bureau 300 - 65 Ouest de Castelnau   Montreal, QC H2R 2W3
V: (514) 278-0807

Association of Visual Language Interpreters of New Brunswick
P.O. Box 22029   Saint John, NB E2K 3A1
V: (506) 652-2839   E-mail: blackgin@nbnet.nb.ca

Maritimes Association of Professional Sign Language Interpreters
P.O. Box 2625, Halifax Central   Halifax, NS B3J 3P7
V: (902) 542-1647   E-mail: mandymacdonald@hotmail.com

Newfoundland & Labrador Interpreter Services
220 Lemarchant Road, Suite 505   St. John's, NF A1E 2H8
TTY: (709) 753-5620   V: (709) 753-5621
Fax: (709) 753-5682   E-mail: nlis@nfld.com

EDUCATIONAL PROGRAMS

Deaf Children's Society of BC
7355 Canada Way   Burnaby, BC V3N 4Z6
TTY: (604) 525-9390   V: (604) 525-6056
Fax: (604) 525-7307   E-mail: deafchildren@infomatch.com

Provincial School for the Deaf – British Columbia
5455 Rumble Street   Burnaby, BC V5J 2B7
TTY: (604) 664-8563   V: (604) 664-8560
Fax: (604) 664-8561   E-mail: info@south.sd41.bc.ca

148

QUIET JOURNEY

Alberta School for the Deaf
6240-113 Street   Edmonton, AB   T6H 3L2
TTY/V: (780) 439-3323
Fax: (780) 435-0385   E-mail: abschdeaf@epsb.edmonton.ab.ca

Saskatchewan Deaf Children's Society Inc.
2209 Ewart Avenue   Saskatoon, SK   S7J 1Y1
TTY/V: (306) 343-9611

Manitoba School for the Deaf
242 Stradford Street   Winnipeg, MB   R2Y 2C9
TTY/V: (204) 945-8934
Fax: (204) 945-1767   E-mail: mbsdeaf@minet.gov.mb.ca

Sign Talk Centre
285 Pembina Highway, Room 224   Winnipeg, MB   R3L 2E1
TTY: (204) 475-8914   V: (204) 475-8906
Fax: (204) 475-9980
Early Start (Home Visitor)
TTY: (204) 284-9781

Centre Jules Leger (French program)
281, Avenue Lanark   Ottawa, ON   K1Z 6R8
TTY: (613) 761-9302   V: (613) 761-9300 ext. 269
Fax: (613) 761-9301   E-mail: andre.duguay@edu.gov.on.ca

Ernest C. Drury School for the Deaf
255 Ontario Street South   Milton, ON   L9T 2M5
TTY: (905) 878-7195   V: (905) 878-2851
Fax: (905) 878-1354   E-mail: ecdrury@edu.gov.on.ca

Happy Hands Preschool – Bob Rumball Centre for the Deaf
2395 Bayview Avenue   North York, ON   M2L 1A2
TTY: (416) 449-8859   V: (416) 449-9651
Fax: (416) 449-8881

Metropolitan Toronto School for the Deaf
43 Millwood Road   Toronto, ON   M4S 1J6
TTY/V: (416) 393-0630
Fax: (416) 393-1888   E-mail: bdooley@bobrumball.org

149

Joanne S. Cripps

Robarts School for the Deaf
P.O. Box 7300, 1090 Highbury Avenue   London, ON   N5Y 4V9
TTY/V: (519) 453-4400   Fax: (519) 453-7943

Sir James Whitney School for the Deaf
350 Dundas Street West   Belleville, ON   K8P 1B2
TTY/V: (613) 967-2823   Fax: (613) 967-4644

MacKay Centre
3500 Decarie Blve.   Montreal, QC   H4A 3J5
TTY: (514) 482-0487   V: (514) 482-0500
Fax: (514) 482-4536   E-mail: jkelly@mackayctr.org

Atlantic Provinces Special Education Authority
5940 South Street   Halifax, NS   B3H 1S6
TTY/V: (902) 424-8500   Fax: (902) 424-0543
E-mail: dhh@apsea.ca   Web site: www.apsea.ca

Service Agencies

The Canadian Hearing Society
Head Office – 271 Spadina Road   Toronto, ON   M5R 2V3
TTY: 416-964-0340   V: 416-964-9595

Assistive Devices Program – Ministry of Health
7 Overlea Blvd., 6th Floor   Toronto, ON   M4H 1Z8
TTY: 1-800-268-6023

Bob Rumball Association of the Deaf
2395 Bayview Avenue   North York, ON   M2L 1A2
TTY/V: 416-447-2378   Fax: 416-449-8881

Family Network for Deaf Children
P.O. Box 50075, South Slope RPO   Burnaby, BC   V5J 1X9
TTY: (604) 538-2866   V: (604) 538-2866
Fax: (604) 538-2866

Hands on Summer Camp Society - Elizabeth Buckley School
795 Gladiola   Victoria, BC   V8Z 2T2
Fax: (250) 727-2215   E-mail: shorebreez@ampsc.com

QUIET JOURNEY

Connect Society – Deafness, Education, Advocacy & Family (DEAF Services)
11342 127 Street   Edmonton, AB   T5M 0T8
TTY: (780) 454-9581   V: (780) 454-9581
Fax: (780) 447-5820

Moncton Hearing Impaired Council Inc.
236 St. George Street   Moncton, NB   E1C 1W1
TTY: (506) 859-6101   V: (506) 859-2979
Fax: (506) 856-5060   E-mail: mhic@nbnet.nb.ca

St. John Deaf and Hard of Hearing Services, Inc.
646 Fairville Blvd., Suite 303   St. John, NB   E2M 4Y7
TTY: (506) 634-8037   V: (506) 633-0599
Fax: (506) 652-3382   E-mail: sjdhhs@nb.sympatico.ca

Newfoundland Coordinating Council on Deafness
P.O. Box 21313   St. John's, NF   A1A 5G6
TTY: (709) 576-4908   V: (709) 576-4592
Fax: (709) 576-7501   E-mail: nccd@sympatico.nf.ca

Deafness Advocacy Association Nova Scotia
1660 Hollis Street, Suite 803   Halifax, NS   B3J 1V7
TTY: (902) 425-0119   V: (902) 425-0240
Fax: (902) 429-9312   E-mail: daans@ns.sympatico.ca

Deaf Connect: Deaf E-mail Directory   www.deafconnect.com
(over 11,000 listings from around the world)

BOOKS, MAGAZINE ARTICLES AND VIDEOS

Baker-Shenk, Charlotte and Dennis Cokely, *American Sign Language: A Teacher's Resource Text on Grammar and Culture* (Washington, DC: Gallaudet University Press, 1991).

Carbin, Clifton F., *Deaf Heritage in Canada: A Distinctive, Diverse and Enduring Culture* (Whitby: McGraw-Hill Ryerson, 1996).

Carbin, Clifton F., "Ontario's New ASL/LSQ Law – Pah!" Article in *Gallaudet Today*, Winter issue 1993-94.

JOANNE S. CRIPPS

Klima E. and Ursulla Bellugi, *The Signs of Language* (Cambridge, MA: Harvard University Press, 1979).

Mahshie, Shawn Neal, *Educating Deaf Children Bilingually: With Insights and Applications from Sweden and Denmark* (Washington, DC: Gallaudet University Press, 1995).

Padden, Carol and Tom Humphries, *Deaf in America: Voices from a Culture* (Cambridge, MA: Harvard University Press, 1988).

Stokoe, William, *Sign Language Structure* (Silver Spring, MD: Lindstock Press, 1960).

Valli, Clayton and Ceil Lucas, *Linguistics of American Sign Language* (Washington, DC: Gallaudet University Press, 1995).

Woodward, James, "Implications for Sociolinguistics Research Among the Deaf," *Sign Language Studies* 1:1-7, 1972.

"Freckles and Popper" videotape series plus *Guide for Parents and Teachers*. These illustrate the richness of Deaf culture and ASL by using examples of ASL literature as well as English literature translated into ASL. Available at the Canadian Cultural Society of the Deaf bookstore.

For more information on cultural and linguistic incorporation, community participation, and advocacy-oriented evaluation mentioned on page 120, see "Denial of Voice: The Suppression of Deaf Children's Language in Canadian Schools" in *Heritage Languages: The Development and Denial of Canada's Linguistic Resources* by Jim Cummins and Marcel Danesi (Toronto: Our Schools? Our Selves Education Foundation/Garamond Press, 1990).

PERMISSIONS AND COPYRIGHT INFORMATION

The letter on pages xi and xii is reprinted from *Eye to Eye*, published by Deaf Children's Society, Vancouver, B.C. October 28, 1998. It is reprinted with permission of Mr. and Mrs. Feanny.

The poem on page xix is reprinted from *Poetry to Greet the Heart II* (Conestoga, Ontario: Hendershot Media Services, 1984). Permission granted by Marlene Stephens.

The excerpt on page 2 is from *Silent Observer* by Christy MacKinnon (Washington, DC: Gallaudet University Press, 1993). Reprinted with permission of the publisher.

The poems on pages 48-50, 62 and 110 are from *Sounds of the Soul: An Anthology of Poetry by Deaf Canadians* (Edmonton: Canadian Cultural Society of the Deaf, 1997). They are reprinted with permission.

The excerpt on page 74 is from "Literacy, Gateway to Fulfillment," special issue of *UNESCO Courier*, June 1980, published in *Feliciter* Magazine, Vol. 45 No. 5, 1999, page 302. It is reprinted with permission.

The excerpt on page 92 is from *Deaf Heritage in Canada* by Clifton F. Carbin (Whitby: McGraw-Hill Ryerson, 1996). It is reprinted with permission.